KnockoutJS by Example

Develop rich, interactive, and real-world web
applications using knockout.js

Adnan Jaswal

BIRMINGHAM - MUMBAI

KnockoutJS by Example

First published: September 2015

Production reference: 1280915

Published by Packt Publishing Ltd.
Livery Place
35 Livery Street
Birmingham B3 2PB, UK.

ISBN 978-1-78528-854-8

www.packtpub.com

Credits

Author
Adnan Jaswal

Reviewers
Taswar Bhatti
Scott Durow
Magesh Kuppan

Commissioning Editor
Sarah Crofton

Acquisition Editor
Vivek Anantharaman

Content Development Editor
Divij Kotian

Technical Editor
Shivani Kiran Mistry

Copy Editor
Swati Priya

Project Coordinator
Nikhil Nair

Proofreader
Safis Editing

Indexer
Monica Ajmera Mehta

Graphics
Disha Haria

Production Coordinator
Arvindkumar Gupta

Cover Work
Arvindkumar Gupta

About the Author

Adnan Jaswal is technologist with vast knowledge and experience in technology consultancy, solution architecture, and software development. He has designed and developed software for government, education, financial, cyber security, logistics, and aviation industries. He believes in the digital revolution and the power it possesses to change the way people and businesses interact with technology. He is passionate about JavaScript technologies and views them as an enabler of digital change.

He has worked for companies such as CA Technologies and Object Consulting. He currently works, as a manager, for one of the big four professional services networks. His role involves technology consulting, architecting, leading teams, developing software, and helping clients respond to digital disruption.

He lives in Melbourne, Australia, with his wife and two children. He can be found on LinkedIn at `https://www.linkedin.com/in/adnanjaswal`.

Acknowledgment

I would like to thank the team of editors, proof readers, and designers who contributed to the quality of this book. My special thanks goes to the technical reviewers of this book for identifying mistakes and suggesting improvements.

To my teachers and mentors, thank you for contributing to my knowledge and experience. I would also like to extent my appreciation to all my colleagues and peers. I enjoy our discussions and collaborations, and they have helped me with the content of this book.

Special thanks also goes to all my family and friends for sharing my happiness and supporting me when I started this project.

To my beautiful children, Heba and Zaki, thank you for the understanding on those days when I was away writing this book. You both bring me so much joy and make me smile every single day. You missed out on daddy time while I was writing this book and I will try my best to make it up.

Finally, to my lovely wife Sadia, thank you for your love and support as I fit the writing schedule into our already overly busy life. You took on additional duties every weekend I had to go write this book. The hard work you put in and the motivation you have is my inspiration. This book has been a long journey for all of us and I could not have done it without you.

About the Reviewers

Taswar Bhatti is a system architect at Gemalto, an international digital security company in Ottawa, Canada. He has been working in the software industry for more than 15 years. He focuses on building secure, highly-distributed, and scalable solutions.

He is also the author of *Instant Automapper, Packt Publishing*. He regularly speaks at meetups and code camps, and blogs on http://taswar.zeytinsoft.com. You can follow him on Twitter @taswarbhatti.

> I would like to thank my wife, Nilay Ertemur Bhatti, and my children, Onur and Sevin Bhatti, for all the love and support.

Scott Durow is an experienced software architect and technologist with a passion for enabling business transformation through the Microsoft technologies. By combining his detailed technical knowledge with a clear grasp of wider commercial issues, he is able to identify and implement practical solutions to complex business challenges.

His software engineering background has moved him through assembly language device driver programming and industrial control systems into enterprise business software, with work experiences in Europe, North America, and Japan. He is a Microsoft Dynamics CRM MVP and the principle author of the open source project, www.SparkleXRM.com.

He lives near the University of Oxford in the UK with his wife, Kerrie, and three children. To read more about his latest projects, you can visit his blog at scottdurow.develop1.net. You can also follow him on Twitter at @ScottDurow.

Magesh Kuppan is a freelance trainer and consultant with 18 years of experience. In his previous incarnation as an architect, he built desktop applications, web applications, data services, and rich internet applications/single page applications for one of the largest financial organizations in the U.S. Currently, he is conducting training programs on most of the JavaScript frameworks/libraries and server-side application development using Node.js for major organizations.

He was also a technical reviewer for *Knockout Essentials*, *Packt Publishing*.

> This is dedicated to my son, Guru Raghav, who makes everyday a beautiful experience.

www.PacktPub.com

Support files, eBooks, discount offers, and more

For support files and downloads related to your book, please visit www.PacktPub.com.

Did you know that Packt offers eBook versions of every book published, with PDF and ePub files available? You can upgrade to the eBook version at www.PacktPub.com and as a print book customer, you are entitled to a discount on the eBook copy. Get in touch with us at service@packtpub.com for more details.

At www.PacktPub.com, you can also read a collection of free technical articles, sign up for a range of free newsletters and receive exclusive discounts and offers on Packt books and eBooks.

https://www2.packtpub.com/books/subscription/packtlib

Do you need instant solutions to your IT questions? PacktLib is Packt's online digital book library. Here, you can search, access, and read Packt's entire library of books.

Why subscribe?

- Fully searchable across every book published by Packt
- Copy and paste, print, and bookmark content
- On demand and accessible via a web browser

Free access for Packt account holders

If you have an account with Packt at www.PacktPub.com, you can use this to access PacktLib today and view 9 entirely free books. Simply use your login credentials for immediate access.

Table of Contents

Preface

JavaScript technologies are playing a much larger role in modern web applications. These application are expected to be rich, interactive, responsive, modular, and maintainable. The applications are often required to redraw parts of the user interface. The data and business logic must be kept separate from the presentation in order to develop modular and maintainable web applications that are interactive and provide a richer user experience. The data and the presentation could then be bound in a way that updates to one would update the other. Similarly, the business logic could be bound to events triggered by the presentation. Developing applications on this design in pure JavaScript can be complex and time-consuming. It becomes evident, to most developers, that a library is required that allows the development of modern web applications without getting into the complexities of binding data, business logic, and presentation. Knockout is one such library.

Knockout is an open source JavaScript library. It reduces the complexities of JavaScript and HTML development by following the stated design principle and implementing the Model-View-View Model (MVVM) design pattern.

One of the best ways to learn a software development technology is by example. Keeping this in mind, my intent has been to provide a practical and hands on learning experience featuring real-world projects. I have drawn on my experience as a software designer and developer to provide you with a practical guide. The inspiration for the content and examples in this book come from my years of experience in developing web applications using JavaScript and, in particular, developing applications using Knockout for a leading financial institution.

If you are new to Knockout, this book is a hands-on guide for you to start creating web applications. With its iterative approach, sample code, and screenshots, this book will take you on a journey of discovering the power of Knockout.

If you are an experienced Knockout developer, this book will give you practical solutions to real-world problems. With advanced topics such as building complex navigations, securing web applications, building services for CRUD operations, and using third party APIs, this book will be your go-to reference.

What this book covers

Chapter 1, Getting Started, covers the basic concepts and patterns that help us understand how Knockout works. It explores the key features of Knockout, including declarative binding, automatic UI refresh, dependency tracking, and templating. The second half of the chapter takes you through building your first Knockout application—an address book.

Chapter 2, Creating a To-do List Application, takes you through building a to-do list application. The application's features include adding, viewing, deleting, sorting, and completing tasks. It also includes features to set the priority on tasks and view the number of total and completed tasks.

Chapter 3, Creating an Online Customer Registration Form, walks you through building a customer registration form. The information captured by the form includes personal information, contact details, residential and postal addresses, and credit card information. The application demonstrates Knockout's ability to create dynamic forms.

Chapter 4, Adding Validation to the Customer Registration Form, describes how to add validation to the form that we built in the previous chapter. It explores two ways of applying validation: using custom extenders and the Knockout validation plugin.

Chapter 5, Creating a Customer Banking Portal, is the first chapter in a series of three that walks you through building a customer banking portal for MyBank. It lets you set up the navigation for the application, display users' contact details, their accounts and associated transactions, and their personal information as well.

Chapter 6, Enhancing the Customer Banking Portal, adds new features to the customer banking portal that we built in the previous chapter. This chapter helps you add features to allow the users to update their personal information and transfer funds between their accounts using a wizard component.

Chapter 7, Securing the Customer Banking Portal, explores the common token-based authentication mechanisms used in modern web applications. It walks you through securing the customer banking portal using token-based authentication.

Chapter 8, Building an Editable Products Grid with CRUD Operations, walks you through building an editable products grid application. The application integrates with a server through RESTful web services. Its features include displaying, deleting, adding, and updating products.

Chapter 9, Using Google Maps APIs with Knockout, walks you through building a map application using the Google Maps APIs. The application gives the users the ability to enter address information with autocomplete predictions, based on partial address input, and displays detailed address information. It also renders a map, places markers based on the addresses selected, and displays the route between the two markers.

What you need for this book

In order to start coding along the examples and running the sample applications that come with this book, you need a device with internet connectivity so that you can download the libraries used in the examples as well as the sample code. You can use your preferred editor or development environment to write the code and start developing web applications. You also require one of the major browsers to run the applications.

Who this book is for

This book is intended for designers and developers who want to learn how to use the Knockout library to develop rich, interactive, and modular web applications. This book will help you master both the basic and the advanced features of Knockout. The book assumes no prior knowledge of the Knockout library, but basic familiarity with HTML, CSS, and JavaScript would be helpful. The book is targeted towards readers who are inspired by the idea of hands-on learning. The sample real-world applications in this book will take you on a journey of building applications that range from basic level all the way to advance.

Conventions

In this book, you will find a number of text styles that distinguish between different kinds of information. Here are some examples of these styles and an explanation of their meaning.

Code words in text, database table names, folder names, filenames, file extensions, pathnames, dummy URLs, user input, and Twitter handles are shown as follows: "The `retrieveContact` function, which is used to retrieve a contact from the server-side."

A block of code is set as follows:

```
var contact = {
    id: 1,
    name: 'John',
    phoneNumber: '00 11 000000'
};
```

When we wish to draw your attention to a particular part of a code block, the relevant lines or items are set in bold:

```
/* the model */
var member = {
    accounts: ko.observableArray(),
    selectedAccount: ko.observable(),
    selectedAccountTransactions: ko.observableArray([])
};
```

New terms and **important words** are shown in bold. Words that you see on the screen, for example, in menus or dialog boxes, appear in the text like this: "Open the application in the browser and try hitting **Submit** without entering any information in the form fields."

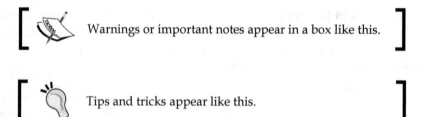

Warnings or important notes appear in a box like this.

Tips and tricks appear like this.

Reader feedback

Feedback from our readers is always welcome. Let us know what you think about this book—what you liked or disliked. Reader feedback is important for us as it helps us develop titles that you will really get the most out of.

To send us general feedback, simply e-mail feedback@packtpub.com, and mention the book's title in the subject of your message.

If there is a topic that you have expertise in and you are interested in either writing or contributing to a book, see our author guide at www.packtpub.com/authors.

Customer support

Now that you are the proud owner of a Packt book, we have a number of things to help you to get the most from your purchase.

License

All code examples, whether in the book or downloaded from your account at http://www.packtpub.com are released under the terms of MIT license as stated here:

Copyright (c) Adnan Jaswal, 2015

Permission is hereby granted, free of charge, to any person obtaining a copy of this software and associated documentation files (the "Software"), to deal in the Software without restriction, including without limitation the rights to use, copy, modify, merge, publish, distribute, sublicense, and/or sell copies of the Software, and to permit persons to whom the Software is furnished to do so, subject to the following conditions:

The above copyright notice and this permission notice shall be included in all copies or substantial portions of the Software.

THE SOFTWARE IS PROVIDED "AS IS", WITHOUT WARRANTY OF ANY KIND, EXPRESS OR IMPLIED, INCLUDING BUT NOT LIMITED TO THE WARRANTIES OF MERCHANTABILITY, FITNESS FOR A PARTICULAR PURPOSE AND NONINFRINGEMENT. IN NO EVENT SHALL THE AUTHORS OR COPYRIGHT HOLDERS BE LIABLE FOR ANY CLAIM, DAMAGES OR OTHER LIABILITY, WHETHER IN AN ACTION OF CONTRACT, TORT OR OTHERWISE, ARISING FROM, OUT OF OR IN CONNECTION WITH THE SOFTWARE OR THE USE OR OTHER DEALINGS IN THE SOFTWARE.

Downloading the example code

You can download the example code files from your account at http://www.
packtpub.com for all the Packt Publishing books you have purchased. If you
purchased this book elsewhere, you can visit http://www.packtpub.com/support
and register to have the files e-mailed directly to you.

Errata

Although we have taken every care to ensure the accuracy of our content, mistakes
do happen. If you find a mistake in one of our books—maybe a mistake in the text or
the code—we would be grateful if you could report this to us. By doing so, you can
save other readers from frustration and help us improve subsequent versions of this
book. If you find any errata, please report them by visiting http://www.packtpub.
com/submit-errata, selecting your book, clicking on the **Errata Submission Form**
link, and entering the details of your errata. Once your errata are verified, your
submission will be accepted and the errata will be uploaded to our website or added
to any list of existing errata under the Errata section of that title.

To view the previously submitted errata, go to https://www.packtpub.com/books/
content/support and enter the name of the book in the search field. The required
information will appear under the **Errata** section.

Piracy

Piracy of copyrighted material on the Internet is an ongoing problem across all
media. At Packt, we take the protection of our copyright and licenses very seriously.
If you come across any illegal copies of our works in any form on the Internet, please
provide us with the location address or website name immediately so that we can
pursue a remedy.

Please contact us at copyright@packtpub.com with a link to the suspected
pirated material.

We appreciate your help in protecting our authors and our ability to bring you
valuable content.

Questions

If you have a problem with any aspect of this book, you can contact us at
questions@packtpub.com, and we will do our best to address the problem.

1
Getting Started

Knockout is an open source JavaScript library that lets you develop rich, interactive, and modular web applications. It does this in a manner that reduces complexities of JavaScript and HTML development and allows us to develop highly scalable, testable, and maintainable web applications.

Knockout provides the ability to bind HTML elements to a data model. The binding is two-way, which means that any change to the data is reflected in the HTML elements and any change to the HTML elements is reflected in the data. Knockout implements two-way binding using the **Model-View-View Model** (**MVVM**) design pattern. You will learn more about this pattern in the next section.

Knockout is a pure JavaScript library and is not dependent on other low-level JavaScript libraries such as jQuery or Prototype. Libraries such as jQuery can be used in conjunction with Knockout to provide richer features to your application such as making AJAX calls, providing animation to HTML elements, or providing event handling for custom user interface components.

Knockout supports all major browsers. A list of supported browsers can be found on the Knockout's website at `http://knockoutjs.com/`.

This chapter covers the following topics:

- Understanding the MVVM design pattern: We will explore the MVVM pattern and how it is implemented using knockout.js
- Key features of Knockout: We will look at the key features of knockout.js

- Understanding the module pattern: We will explore the module pattern and see how it can be used to give structure to your Knockout application
  - ° Building your first application: We will build the first application and learn where to download knockout.js from and how to set up the development environment
  - ° Defining data model and applying data bindings: We will also learn the basics of defining the data model and applying data bindings
  - ° Applying styles to our application using Bootstrap
- Taking a look at some useful resources

Understanding the MVVM design pattern

Knockout implements the MVVM design pattern. It is imperative to understand the basic concept behind MVVM before we dive into Knockout. This will help us grasp how two-way binding is implemented in Knockout and what are its benefits.

MVVM is a design pattern that lets you decouple your UI elements from your application logic and data. It lets you define data binding to link the UI elements to the data. The data bindings provides loose coupling and keeps the data in sync with the UI elements. The MVVM pattern provides clear separation of concerns between UI elements, application logic, and the data.

The three main components of this pattern are:

The model

The model is a domain object, which holds the data and domain-specific logic. An example of a model could be of a contact in an address book, containing contact ID, name, and phone number. The following is an example of a contact model in JavaScript:

```
var contact = {
    id: 1,
    name: 'John',
    phoneNumber: '00 11 000000'
};
```

The model should not contain any application logic such as service calls. The model can contain business-specific logic that is independent of the UI. Separating business logic from UI makes the code more maintainable and testable.

The contact object in the given example is declared as an object literal, which uses **Java Script Object Notation (JSON)**. It is important to familiarize yourself with this notation if you are not. You can find more on this topic at http://json.org/.

The view model

The view model holds the model and any application logic such as adding or removing data or making service calls to retrieve or storing data from server-side data repositories. The following is an example of a view model that holds a contact and provides method to retrieve the contact from a server-side data repository:

```
var contactViewModel = {
  var contact = {
    id: 1,
    name: 'John',
    phoneNumber: '00001111'
  };

  Var retrieveContact = function (){
    /* logic to retrieve contact form server side data repository
    */
  };

  Var updateContact = function (newPhoneNumber){
    /* logic to update the contact with new phone number */
  };
};
```

The view model itself does not have any concept of the HTML elements, button-click event, or how the data in the model should be displayed. It simply holds the data model and a set of actions in the form of functions that manipulate the data.

In the preceding example, contactViewModel holds the contact model. It also has two functions that are used to manipulate the contact model. The retrieveContact function, which is used to retrieve a contact from the server-side, and the updateContact function, which is used to update the contact with a new phone number.

The view

The view is what the end user sees and interacts with on the screen. The view is a representation of the data contained in the model. The view also provides a mechanism to interact with the model. In our example, the model contains a contact. The view can display the contact and provide HTML elements such as buttons to retrieve and update the contact.

In Knockout, the view is the HTML with data bindings that link the view to the view model. The following HTML displays the contact name and phone number:

```
The phone number for <span data-bind="text: name"></span> is
<span data-bind="text: phoneNumber"></span>
<button data-bind="click: retrieveContact">Load Contact</button>
```

In the preceding example, the contact name and phone number are being displayed using the text binding. Click binding is used to link the `Load Contact` button to `retrieveContact` function in our view model. We will explore bindings in much more detail later on.

The following figure depicts the relationship between view, model, and view model:

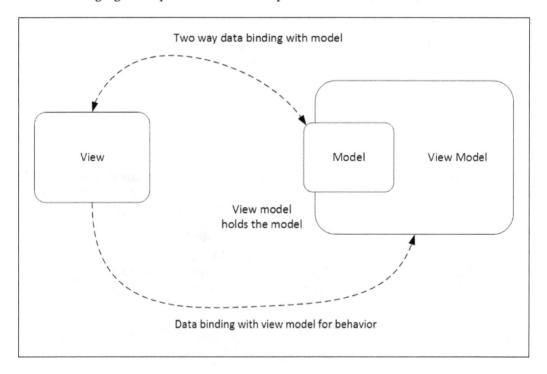

In the preceding figure, the view model holds the state of the model and provides behavior to the view. The view binds with the model and this keeps the view and the model in sync. The view also binds with the view model for operations, for example, the behavior to load contacts. The view model uses the model to manipulate the data. For example, the `retrieveContact` function retrieves a contact and sets it in the model.

The key features of Knockout

In this section, we will explore some of the key features of Knockout. It is important to understand these features and their basic syntax before we dive into working examples.

Declarative bindings

Knockout provides a way to link the model and view model with the view using a declarative binding mechanism. The bindings are declared in HTML. The following is an example of a simple text binding:

```
The phone number for <span data-bind="text: name></span> is
0000111
```

Let's explore the data binding syntax. The bindings are declared using the data-bind attribute on an HTML element. The value of this attribute has two elements, which are separated by a colon. The two elements are name and a value.

The name specifies the type of binding. This should match a registered binding handler. A **binding handler** is an object that contains the code to bind the HTML element to our model. Knockout provides a number of useful binding handlers. A custom binding handler can be created and registered with Knockout if none of the out-of-the-box handlers meet your specific requirements. In most cases, the out-of-the-box handlers will do the job.

 Knockout will ignore the binding without any error if the name does not match any of the registered binding handlers. Check the name if the binding does not appear to be working!

The value can be an attribute from the model or any valid JavaScript expression. In the preceding example for contact, we used a text binding with the value, and the name. The value in this case comes from the model.

Here is an example of a binding using a JavaScript expression:

```
The phone number for <span data-bind="text:
retrieveContactName()></span> is 0000111
```

In this example, the text value is evaluated by calling the `retrieveContactName` JavaScript function.

 Knockout will throw an error and stop processing the bindings if the value is an invalid expression or if it references an undefined variable.

You can include multiple bindings in the `data-bind` attribute, with each binding separated by a comma. Adding a visible binding to our weather forecast example will make it look similar to this:

```
The phone number for <span data-bind="text: name, css:
favourite"></span> is 0000111
```

In the preceding example, the text for the `span` element will come from the `name` attribute in our model. The `css` binding will determine the CSS class to be applied, based on the `favourite` attribute in our model for the `span` element.

 You can include any number of spaces, tabs, or newlines in your binding syntax. Use this to arrange your bindings to make them more readable!

In more advance usage, the binding can also be a parameter for another binding. Here is an example in which the template binding takes the `foreach` binding as a parameter:

```
<tbody data-bind="template: {name: 'contact-template', foreach:
contacts}">
```

As mentioned earlier, Knockout provides a number of very useful binding handlers that come out of the box. Knockout documentation divides these binding handlers in to three categories:

- **Controlling text and appearance**: As the name suggests, these binding handlers control the text and the styling of the UI elements. Examples of binding handlers in this category include `text` and `css`. We used these bindings as examples earlier in this section.

- **Flow control**: These binding handlers provide control structures such as loops and conditions. The `foreach` and `if` binding handlers fall under this category. We will explore these bindings in more detail in the coming sections.

- **Working with form fields**: Capturing data with forms is one of the most basic requirements in web applications. Binding handlers in this category provide the functionality to work with form fields. Some of the examples include `click`, `value`, and `submit` binding handlers. We will learn more about bindings in this category in *Chapter 3, Creating an Online Customer Registration Form* and *Chapter 4, Adding Validation to the Customer Registration Form*.

Automatic UI refresh

Automatic UI refresh is a very useful feature of Knockout. This feature is based on the concept of two-way binding between the view and view model. Whenever the data in the model changes, it is reflected in the UI. When the input fields in the UI change, it updates the underlying data.

This feature reduces the amount of code and complexity by many folds. Those who are accustomed to writing event handlers in JavaScript to connect data with UI fields and vice versa would surely appreciate this feature. Implementing this in jQuery is definitely easier than developing this in pure JavaScript, but it does not compare with Knockout.

The examples in the previous section for data binding and view produces a one-way binding between the UI and model. Updating the value in the UI field will update the data in the model. To make this binding work both ways, you have to declare the attributes in your model as observables.

Observables are objects that notify their subscribers of any change. Let's apply observables to our contact model:

```
var contact = {
    id: ko.observable(1),
    name: ko.observable('John'),
    phoneNumber: ko.observable('00001111')
};
```

By declaring the attributes in your model as observable object, you have activated the two-way binding. You do not have to make any change to the data bindings or view.

Since observables are functions, you can no longer access the attribute in the standard way. To read the value of our name observable, we execute it as a function like this:

```
contact.name();
```

To change the value of our name observable to `Mary`, simply pass the new value as an argument to the name function as follows:

```
contact.name('Mary');
```

We mentioned that observables notify their subscribers of any change. When we use observables with data binding, the binding registers itself to be notified when the observable changes value. When the value of the observable changes, the binding automatically updates the UI element.

You can also explicitly subscribe to observables, have observables with values that are computed, or even delay change notification. We will learn more about these later on in the book.

Dependency tracking

Dependency tracking is one of the most exciting features of Knockout. Dependency tracking is based on observables and their subscribers. When Knockout runs for the first time, it evaluates the initial value of each observable and sets up the subscriptions. The subscribers get notified when the observable gets updated with a new value.

Dependency tracking also works for computed observables. Computed observables are the observables that are dependent on one or more other observables. The value of the computed observable is updated every time the value of one of its dependencies changes.

Let's extend our contact model to add first and last name:

```
var contact = {
  id: ko.observable(1),
  firstName: ko.observable('John'),
  lastName: ko.observable('Jones'),
  phoneNumber: ko.observable('00001111')
};
```

Now that we have added observables for first and last name, let's add a computed observable for full name:

```
var contact = {
id: ko.observable(1),
  firstName: ko.observable('John'),
  lastName: ko.observable('Jones'),
```

```
    fullName: ko.computed(function() {
      return this.firstName() + " " + this.lastName();
    }, this),
    phoneNumber: ko.observable('00001111')
  };
```

The `fullName` attribute will return the concatenated first name and last name. Knockout will compute the value of `fullName` every time the values of either first or last name change.

Dependency tracking allows us to build complex yet sophisticated models that have a set of key attributes and the effects of changing the attributes rippled across the view. Dependency tracking in Knockout is also dynamic. This means that we can have the full name initially dependent on first and last name and then at runtime, add another dependency, say, middle name.

Templating

Templating is another very useful feature of Knockout. Templates are the UI structure that renders a UI, based on the provided elements in the template. Templates are useful when you have a requirement of using the same UI structure multiple times in your application. You should not be expected to cut and paste the same structure every time you plan to use it.

The most basic example of a template is when it is used to repeatedly render a row in a table:

```
<table>
  <thead>
    <tr>
      <th>Contact</th>
      <th>Phone Number</th>
    </tr>
  </thead>
  <tbody data-bind="foreach: contacts">
    <tr>
      <td data-bind="text: name"></td>
      <td data-bind="text: phoneNumber"></td>
    </tr>
  </tbody>
</table>
```

In the preceding example, we are using the `foreach` binding to repeatedly render a table row. The HTML markup within the `tbody` element is used as the template to render each contact. Using templates in this way is only useful with control structures, such as loops and conditions. It is not very useful if you plan to use the template in multiple different locations in your application. This is where named templates are handy.

 The `foreach` binding is the Knockout construct for looping over an array. We will explore `foreach` binding in more details later on.

Let's rewrite our previous example to use a named template:

```
<table>
  <thead>
    <tr>
      <th>Contact</th>
      <th>Phone Number</th>
    </tr>
  </thead>
  <tbody data-bind="template: {name: 'contact-template', foreach:
  contacts}">
  </tbody>
</table>

<script type="text/html" id="contact-template">
  <tr>
    <td data-bind="text: name"></td>
    <td data-bind="text: phoneNumber"></td>
  </tr>
</script>
```

In this example, we extracted the template into a script block and gave it an ID, `contact-template`. We then modified the data binding to add a binding for the template. The template binding takes a name of the template, which is the ID of the script block containing our template. The `foreach` binding is a parameter for the template binding.

Templates in Knockout are both flexible and powerful. You can dynamically choose a template by pointing the `name` attribute of the template to an observable in your model. You can also add a post processing logic to the template by adding the `afterRender` attribute. This attribute can point to a function in your view model that takes the HTML element as a parameter.

Knockout also supports third party templating engines such as `jQuery.tmpl` and Underscore. The examples in this book use native Knockout templates. Native templates are more than adequate for most use case.

Understanding the module pattern and its use with Knockout

In the previous section, we explored the key features of Knockout. We learned the basics of declarative data binding, automated UI refresh, dependency tracking, and templating. Knockout does a really good job of simplifying web application development by providing these features. However, it does not solve the problem of bringing structure to your JavaScript code.

Unlike an object-oriented programming language such as Java or C#, JavaScript does not enforce any particular structure. This is both a blessing and a curse. Blessing in the sense that you can bring your own rules on how to structure your code. This gives you power and flexibility. It can be a curse if you do not follow any structure as in that case, your code base becomes too large and complex. Giving structure to your JavaScript code becomes more and more important as you write complex JavaScript applications. Structuring your JavaScript will make the code more maintainable and readable. It also helps to make the code more testable.

The concept

An elegant yet simple way of giving structure to your JavaScript code is by using the module pattern. It is important to understand the basic concepts behind the module pattern as we will be using this pattern throughout this book. Let's get started with the basic concept.

Central to the module pattern is the concept of a module. A module is a component that encapsulates everything that is required to accomplish a set of related tasks. This includes data as well as behavior. Here is an example of creating a module using the module pattern in JavaScript:

```
(function () {
   /* module code */
}) ( );
```

Let's deconstruct and explore what the preceding code does. Since JavaScript does not provide a construct for creating modules or classes, we use the next best thing—the anonymous function construct. The preceding code constructs and executes an anonymous function. The module code inside this function maintains privacy from the outside world. This is because creating a function creates a new scope. The module code also maintains its state throughout the life cycle of the module. Notice the parenthesis ( ) at the end of our function. These parenthesis execute our anonymous function straight after creation and creates our module.

 By convention, the modules are named with uppercase first letter.

We need a way to namespace our newly created module. This will allow us to access any public attributes that the module might expose:

```
var Module = (function () {
   /* module code */
})( );
```

In the module we defined here, the scope of any attributes or function is confined to the module. You cannot access an attribute that is declared within the module. This is exactly what we want to do—encapsulate everything related to a set of tasks.

Public and private members

If everything is now encapsulated, how does the outside world interact with our module? The answer is a return object with references to attributes and functions that we want to expose to the outside world. With the public and private members defined, the module will look similar to this:

```
var Module = (function () {
   /* private attribute */
   var privateAttribute;

   /* private function */
   var privateFunction = function () {};

   /* public attribute */
   var publicAttribute;

   /* public function */
```

```
  var publicFunction = function () {};

  /* return object with reference to public attributes and
  functions */
  return {
    publicAttribute: publicAttribute,
    publicFunction: publicFunction
  };
})();
```

The scope of the private members, prefixed with the word private, is confined to the module. The public members, prefixed with the word public, are exposed to the outside world through the return object. The return object simply references the public members. We can now access the public members as follows:

```
Module.publicAttribute = 'foo';
Module.publicFunction();
```

Initializing the module

One final element I want to add to my module is a function that initializes the module. Some people like to call it a constructor. Strictly speaking, a constructor is a function that creates an object. It can, however, contain initialization logic. This is not what our function will do. Our function will only initialize the module, hence I won't be calling it a constructor. You can choose any name for your initialization function. I like to call it init. Let's add the init function to our module:

```
var Module = (function () {
  /* private attribute */
  var privateAttribute;
  /* private function */
  var privateFunction = function () {};

  /* public attribute */
  var publicAttribute;

  /* public function */
  var publicFunction = function () {};

  var init = function() {
    /* Module initialization logic*/
  };

  /* fire the init function */
```

```
    init();

    /* return object with reference to public attributes and
    functions */
    return {
      publicAttribute: publicAttribute,
      publicFunction: publicFunction
    };
})();
```

In the preceding example, we can see the init function being declared. The scope of this function is private as it is not exposed by the return object. Declaring the function does not mean that our function will execute when the module is created. We execute the function by calling it after declaration:

```
/* execute the init function */
init();
```

On most occasions, we want to execute our init function after the HTML is fully loaded by the browser and the DOM is ready. This is where jQuery comes handy. We can use a feature provided by jQuery to execute the init function once the HTML is fully loaded and the DOM is ready. This is done by replacing the call init(); with:

```
/* execute the init function once the DOM is ready */
jQuery(init);
```

Passing any function as an argument to the jQuery function executes it once the DOM is ready. In the preceding code, we pass the init function as an argument to the jQuery function.

 The dollar sign, $, is a short hand for jQuery. jQuery() is the same as $().

Using the module with view model

Now that we have learned the basic concepts behind the module pattern, let's declare the contact view model we used earlier as a module:

```
var ContactViewModel = (function () {
  var contact = {
    id: ko.observable(1),
```

```
  name: ko.observable('John'),
  phoneNumber: ko.observable(00001111)
};

Var retrieveContact = function (){
  /* logic to retrieve contact form server side data repository
  */
};

Var updateContact = function (newPhoneNumber){
  /* logic to update the contact with new phone number */
};

var init = function() {
  /* Module initialization logic*/
};

/* execute the init function once the DOM is ready */
$(init);

return {
  contact: contact,
  updateContact: updateContact
};
})();
```

Our preceding module is referenced by `ContactViewModel`. It has a contact model and functions to retrieve and update the contact. It also has an initialization function, which will be executed once the DOM is ready. The module exposes the contact model and the `updateContact` function as public members to the outside world. The retrieve contact function remains private to the module.

Building the address book application

Now that we have a basic understanding of the design patterns we will be using and the key features of Knockout, let's dive into building our first application. Our first application is an address book, which is used to store and display contact details of your family and friends. The application lets you add a contact's name and phone number. The contacts are displayed in a table. This is a simple application that highlights some of the basic features that Knockout has to offer.

We will take an iterative approach in building this and all the other example applications in this book. The idea behind an iterative approach is to build the application in small portions. Each portion will deliver a subset of the features. We will continue to evolve the application until the full application is implemented.

A word on the development environment

You can use any **Integrated Development Environment** (IDE) of your choice or simply use a text editor like notepad or vi to develop the application. I recommend using an IDE as it increases developer productivity by many folds. I use an open source IDE called **eclipse**. You can find out more about eclipse at `http://eclipse.org/`.

Web applications are typically hosted on a web server. You can choose a web server that you are familiar with to host the example applications in this book. The two web server that I recommend are:

- **Apache HTTP Server**: This is the most popular web server on the internet. You can find out more about Apache at `http://httpd.apache.org/`.

- **Node.js HTTP Server**: Node.js has gained popularity in recent times. Find out more about Node.js at `http://nodejs.org/`.

You do not require a web server for developing a pure client-side web application using only HTML, JavaScript, and CSS. You can simply view the HTML files by opening them in a browser from your file system. Most examples in this book do not require a web server for development unless you are planning to host the applications or the application requires a server-side component such as a RESTful API endpoint.

Downloading the libraries

First, we need to download the libraries that we require. The two libraries we require are Knockout and jQuery.

Download Knockout from the Knockout's website at `http://knockoutjs.com/`. This should be a single JavaScript file.

Next, download jQuery from the jQuery's website at `http://jquery.com/`. This should also be a single JavaScript file.

Creating the skeleton

First, we will create the skeleton for our address book application. We will use this skeleton for all the example applications in this book.

 A skeleton is a high-level structure that compiles but does not provide any application features. The skeleton is iteratively evolved into a working application. The skeleton forms a template that provides the basic structure, which can be then used in other applications.

Let's create the folder structure for development by following these steps:

1. Create the `AddressBook` folder. This is the main folder that houses our address book application.

2. Add a `WebContent` folder under the `AddressBook` folder. This folder holds the content that gets published to the web.

3. Add a `javascript` folder under the `WebContent` folder. As the folder name suggests, this folder will contain all our JavaScript files.

Now that we have the folder structure in place, let's add some files to our folders by following these steps:

1. Add the Knockout library that you downloaded to the `javascript` folder.

2. Add the JQuery library that you downloaded to the `javascript` folder.

3. Create the `addressbook.js` file under the `javascript` folder.

4. Create the `addressbook.html` file under the `WebContent` folder.

Following these steps should result a folder structure that looks similar to this:

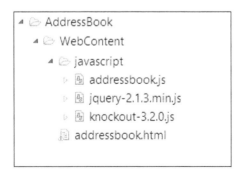

Now that we have created the folder structure, we can add code to our HTML and JavaScript files. Open the `addressbook.html` file and add the following HTML code:

```
<!DOCTYPE HTML>
<html>
  <head>
    <meta http-equiv="Content-Type" content="text/html" />
    <title><!-- add title --></title>
    <!-- the jquery library -->
    <script type="text/javascript"
    src="javascript/jquery-2.1.3.min.js"></script>
    <!-- the knockout library -->
    <script type="text/javascript"
    src="javascript/knockout-3.2.0.js"></script>
    <!-- module for our application -->
    <script type="text/javascript"
    src="javascript/addressbook.js"></script>
  </head>
  <body>
    <!-- add body content -->
  </body>
</html>
```

The file in its current state does not do much. It references Knockout and jQuery libraries from our `javascript` folder. It also references our `addressbook.js` application module.

 Any application modules, such as `addressbook.js`, should always be referenced after the Knockout and jQuery libraries. This is because the application module will use the `ko` and `$` objects defined by these libraries. Make sure that the application module is referenced after these libraries if you get an error, stating that either `ko` or `$` is undefined.

Open the `addressbook.js` file and add the following code; this code defines our empty `AddressBook` module:

```
/* Module for Address Book application */
var AddressBook = function () {

    /* add members here */

    var init = function () {
```

```
    /* add code to initialize this module */
  };

  /* execute the init function when the DOM is ready */
  $(init);

  return {
    /* add members that will be exposed publicly */
  };
}();
```

View the `addressbook.html` file in your browser. The browser should give you a black page, which is not very exciting, but what we have done is created the skeleton for our application. Next, we will start building the application features.

Adding the application features

Our address book application captures, stores, and displays contacts details of our family and friends.

Capturing and storing contacts

Let's develop the functionality to capture and store the contacts. The two pieces of information we want to capture and store is the contact name and phone number. This is defined as a model in our `AddressBook` module. To do this, open the `addressbook.js` file and add the following code:

```
/* add members here */
  var contact = {
  name: ko.observable(),
  phoneNumber: ko.observable()
};
```

The code defines a contact object with two attributes—`name` and `phoneNumber`. The attributes are Knockout observables. We will bind the `contact` object to our HTML input fields to capture user input. Before we add the HTML fields and the binding construct, we need to expose the contact object publicly so that it can be accessed outside our module, for example, by our HTML binding construct. This is done by adding the contact object to the `return` statement of our module. Let's add the `contact` object to the `return` statement. Here is what the code should be:

```
return {
  /* add members that will be exposed publicly */
  contact: contact
};
```

Let's now add the HTML input fields to our view and bind them to our view model. Open `addressbook.html` and the following code in the body of the HTML; take this opportunity to also change the title of the HTML page to something more appropriate like `Knockout: Address Book Example`:

```
<p>Name <input type="text" data-bind="value: AddressBook.contact.name"
/></p>

<p>Phone Number <input type="text" data-bind="value: AddressBook.
contact.phoneNumber" /></p>
```

In the preceding code, we have declared two HTML input fields, one for the contact name and the other for the contact phone number. We also added the binding construct by using `data-bind`. Notice the way we accessed the model. For example, to access the name attribute of the contact, we used the name of our module, `AddressBook`; followed by the name of our model object, `contact`; followed by the name of the attribute, `name`.

The capturing of user input is not complete without a button to indicate that the user has entered a new contact. Add a button to your HTML by inserting the following line after the input text fields:

```
<p><button data-bind="click:
AddressBook.addContact">Add</button></p>
```

The preceding code will add a button to your view with the `Add` label. It also adds a `click` binding. As a result of the click binding, an `addContact` function will get executed when the user clicks on the `Add` button. We have not yet defined the `addContact` method. Let's do this by adding the following code to our view model:

```
var addContact = function () {
console.log("Adding new contact with name: " + contact.name() +"
and phone number: " + contact.phoneNumber());
};
```

The code displays the values of contact name and phone number from the contact object in the browser console. Notice how we access the value of the `name` and `phoneNumber` observables. The `addContact` method needs to be publicly accessible as it is referenced in our view. Let's do this by adding it to the return statement of our module. Our `return` statement should now look similar to this:

```
return {
  /* add members that will be exposed publicly */
  contact: contact,
  addContact: addContact
};
```

We are missing one very important step before we can run what we have developed so far. That step is to activate Knockout. Add the following line of code to the `init` function in our module:

```
var init = function () {
  /* add code to initialize this module */
  ko.applyBindings(AddressBook);
};
```

Here, the `applyBindings` function takes view model as the parameter and applies the bindings declared in our view to the model and behavior, defined in our view model. We pass the view model to the `applyBindings` function by passing our `AddressBook` module.

Now that our application is capturing the contact details, let's develop the functionality to store the contacts. The contacts will be stored using an array. We cannot use the normal JavaScript array as we will need to bind the array to our view in order to display the contacts. Knockout provides a way to construct an array of observables. To make an array of contacts, add the following code to our `AddressModule` below the contact:

```
var contacts = ko.observableArray();
```

The `observableArray` function returns an object, which can track the objects it holds. This means that any subscriber will be notified when an object is added or removed from it.

 The members of the objects that `observableArray` hold, do not become observables. This, however, can be achieved through additional code.

Now that we have declared our contacts array, let's add the contact to our contacts array. Modify the `addContact` function and add the following line of code to push a contact to the contacts array. Your `addContact` function should look similar to this:

```
var addContact = function () {
console.log("Adding new contact with name: " + contact.name() +" and
phone number: " + contact.phoneNumber());

//add the contact to the contacts array
contacts.push({name: contact.name(), phoneNumber: contact.
phoneNumber()});
};
```

Knockout `observableArray` provides useful methods to interact with the array. We have used a method `push`, which insets a new item at the end of the array. We pass a new contact object to the `push` method by creating an object with `name` and `phone` number as attributes. The value of the attributes come from our `name` and `phoneNumber` observables in the contact object.

You may have noticed that the input fields for name and phone numbers retain their values after the add button is clicked and the object is added to the contacts array. This is not for user experience as the user has to clear the inputs before a new contact can be added. To clear the input fields, add the following method to your `AddressBook` module:

```
var clearContact = function () {
  contact.name(null);
  contact.phoneNumber(null);
};
```

Call this method from your `addContact` method after pushing the new contact to the contacts array. The `clearContact` method clears the values of the name and `phoneNumber` observable by setting them to null. The two-way data binding takes care of updating the HTML input fields. You do not have to add the `clearContact` method to the `return` statement of the module as this a private member, which is not required by any other external module or view.

So far, we have:

- Developed our application skeleton
- Created our view with two HTML input text fields for capturing contact name and phone number, and a button to allow user to add a contact
- Created our module with a model for capturing the user input and storing contacts in an array
- Added functionality to add the contact to the contacts array and clear the input fields
- Added declarative binding to our view to bind the HTML input fields to the contact object and the `Add` button to the `addContact` function in our view model
- Activated Knockout by calling the `applyBindings` function in our `init` function

Let's run our application and see what happens. Open `addressbook.html` in a browser. Don't forget to open the console window of the browser. Try adding a contact.

You can open the console window in Chrome by hitting the *F12* key and selecting **Console** in the menu bar.

The application should look similar to this:

Displaying contacts

The next application feature we will add to our address book application is displaying the list of contacts in a table. We will use the HTML table element with `foreach` binding. Let's get straight into it.

Open the `addressbook.html` file and add the following code under the input HTML fields:

```
<table>
  <thead>
    <tr>
      <th>Name</th>
      <th>Phone Number</th>
    </tr>
  </thead>
  <tbody data-bind="foreach: AddressBook.contacts">
    <tr>
      <td data-bind="text: name"></td>
      <td data-bind="text: phoneNumber"></td>
    </tr>
  </tbody>
</table>
```

In the preceding code, we are using the `foreach` binding to repeatedly render a table row of contacts. The `foreach` binding provides a loop construct to display HTML elements based on a template. The HTML markup within the `tbody` element is used as the template to render each contact.

The data binding declaration in the preceding code refers to the contacts array in our module. We have not yet declared the contacts array to be publicly accessible. Make the contacts array publicly accessible by adding it to the return statement of your module. The return statement of `AddressBook` module should look similar to this:

```
return {
    /* add members that will be exposed publicly */
    contact: contact,
    contacts: contacts,
    addContact: addContact
};
```

Downloading the example code

You can download the example code files from your account at `http://www.packtpub.com` for all the Packt Publishing books you have purchased. If you purchased this book elsewhere, you can visit `http://www.packtpub.com/support` and register to have the files e-mailed directly to you.

Run the application by opening `addressbook.html` in a browser. Try adding some contacts. You should now be able to see the newly added contacts displayed in the table. The application should look similar to this:

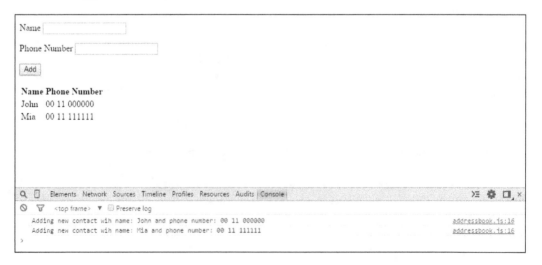

Adding style to your application with Bootstrap

We have added the application features to our address book application, but the application does not look very visually appealing. Let's make it a bit more attractive by adding Bootstrap to our address book application.

 Bootstrap is a popular HTML, CSS, and JavaScript framework for developing web applications. It provides out-of-the-box styles for HTML elements such as labels, buttons, and tables. Find out more about Bootstrap at `http://getbootstrap.com/`.

Follow these steps to download and set up Bootstrap:

1. Download Bootstrap from the Bootstrap website.

2. Create a `bootstrap` folder under `WebContent`.

3. Extract the contents of the download package in the `bootstrap` folder created in the previous step.

Your folder structure should look similar to this:

You are now ready to use Bootstrap. Include the Bootstrap theme in your application by adding the following line to your HTML inside the head element. Your head element should look similar to this:

```
<head>
    <meta http-equiv="Content-Type" content="text/html" />
    <title>Knockout : Address Book Example</title>
    <link rel="stylesheet" href="bootstrap/css/bootstrap.min.css">
    <script type="text/javascript"
    src="javascript/jquery-2.1.3.min.js"></script>
    <script type="text/javascript"
    src="javascript/knockout-3.2.0.js"></script>
    <script type="text/javascript"
    src="javascript/addressbook.js"></script>
</head>
```

You are free to make your own layout and style choices if you are familiar with Bootstrap. If not, you can follow these steps and make the changes to add the Bootstrap styling to your application:

1. Wrap the contents of the HTML body in a div element and give it a class, container.

2. Add a heading using the h1 element just after the body and wrap it in a div element. Give the div element a page-header class like this:

    ```
    <div class="page-header"> <h1>My Address Book</h1></div>
    ```

3. Wrap the HTML input fields and the button in a p element. Remove any p elements that the input fields were previously wrapped in.

4. Add btn and btn-primary classes to the Add button, like this:

    ```
    <button class="btn btn-primary" data-bind="click:
    AddressBook.addContact">Add</button>
    ```

5. Add the table class to the contacts table, like this:

    ```
    <table class="table">
    ```

After making these modifications, your address book application should look, like this:

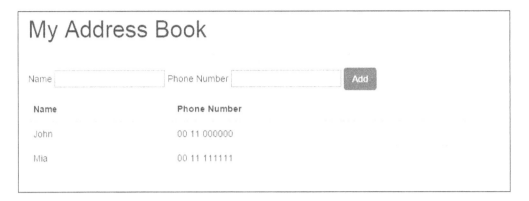

You have successfully completed your first Knockout application! Let's look at some useful resources and summarize what we learned.

Resources

Knockout is a popular open source JavaScript library supported by a vibrant community. The following is a list of some key resources to help you with your journey:

- **Knockout Home**: Download the Knockout library and access document from Knockout home at `http://knockoutjs.com/`

- **Learn Knockout**: Access a set of interactive tutorials to help you quickly get you up and running at `http://learn.knockoutjs.com/`

- **Stack Overflow**: Access Stack Overflow questions and answer site for Knockout at `http://stackoverflow.com/tags/knockout.js/`

- **Knockout GitHub**: Access to source code on GitHub at `https://github.com/knockout/knockout`

- **Google Group**: Access Google group for Knockout at `https://groups.google.com/forum/#!forum/knockoutjs`

Summary

In the first half of this chapter, we covered some basic concepts and patterns that helped us understand how Knockout works. After a brief overview of Knockout, we dived into the MVVM pattern. We explored the concept behind this pattern and saw how it helps in reducing complexities of web application development. We then explored the key features of Knockout that included declarative bindings, automatic UI refresh, dependency tracking, and templating. We looked at the module pattern and learned how we can use it to give structure to our Knockout application.

In the second half of this chapter, we built our first Knockout application. The application was an address book, which was used to store and display contact details of your family and friends. The application let you add a contact name and phone number. The contacts were displayed in a table.

This chapter provided the necessary concepts, pattern, and skeleton code to start developing more complex applications, which follow in the next chapters.

2
Creating a To-do List Application

In the previous chapter, we built a simple address book application and introduced the skeleton we will be using in this book to develop more complex applications. This chapter will walk you through building a more complex application, a to-do list. This application will build and enhance the concepts learned in the previous chapter.

In this chapter, you will learn how to:

- Work with lists using observable arrays
- Bind input elements such as text fields and dropdown to our model
- Use the `foreach` flow control with templating to render a table
- Control text using the `text` data binding
- Control appearance using the `css` data binding
- Use visible binding to show or hide components
- Sort the list using the sort method of the observable arrays
- Filter the list using the `arrayFilter` method of the `ko.utils` package
- Use computed observables to display dynamically changing data

The to-do list application allows the user to create and manage tasks. The application has the following features:

- Add and view tasks
- Delete a task
- Complete a task
- Set a priority for my tasks
- View the tasks sorted by priority and name
- View the number of total and completed tasks

As mentioned in the previous chapter, we will be taking an iterative approach to building the applications in this book. We will iteratively develop each feature listed earlier until the application evolves into a fully featured one. Each feature will have a corresponding checkpoint folder in the accompanying code. The folders are named as chapter2\checkpoint1, chapter2\checkpoint2, and so on.

Creating the skeleton

We need to create the skeleton before we can start building the application features. Follow the steps given to create the skeleton. You should be familiar with these steps from the previous chapter.

Create the folder structure for development by following these steps.

1. Create the ToDoList folder. This is the main folder that houses our to-do list application.
2. Add a WebContent folder under the ToDoList folder. This folder holds the content that gets published to the web.
3. Add a javascript folder under the WebContent folder. As the folder name suggests, this folder will contain all our JavaScript files.
4. Add bootstrap folder under the WebContent folder. This folder will contain the Bootstrap files.

Now that we have the folder structure in place, let's add the files to our folders by following these steps:

1. Add the Knockout library to the javascript folder.
2. Add the JQuery library to the javascript folder.

3. Add Bootstrap to the `bootstrap` folder.

4. Create the file `todolist.js` under the `javascript` folder.

5. Create the `todolist.html` file under the `WebContent` folder.

Following these preceding steps should result in a folder structure that looks similar to this:

Now that we have created the folder structure, we can add code to our HTML and JavaScript files. Open the `todolist.html` file and add the following HTML code:

```html
<!DOCTYPE HTML>
<html>
  <head>
    <meta http-equiv="Content-Type" content="text/html" />
    <title>Knockout : ToDo List Example</title>

    <link rel="stylesheet" href="bootstrap/css/bootstrap.min.css">

    <script type="text/javascript"
    src="javascript/jquery-2.1.3.min.js"></script>
    <script type="text/javascript"
    src="javascript/knockout-3.2.0.js"></script>
    <script type="text/javascript"
    src="javascript/todolist.js"></script>

  </head>
  <body>
    <div class="container">
      <div class="page-header">
```

```
        <h1>My ToDo List</h1>
      </div>
    </div>
  </body>
</html>
```

The preceding code references the required libraries and displays a page header with the name of our application—My ToDo List. Open the todolist.js file and add the following code. This code defines our empty ToDoList module:

```
/* Module for ToDo List application */
var ToDoList = function () {

  /* add members here */

  var init = function () {
    /* add code to initialize this module */
  };

  /* execute the init function when the DOM is ready */
  $(init);

  return {
    /* add members that will be exposed publicly */
  };
}();
```

View the application in the browser. It should give you a page with the page header. We are now ready to create the functionality to add and view tasks.

Let's get started and build the first feature of our to-do list application.

Adding and viewing tasks

The first feature of our to-do application is to give the users the ability to create and view tasks. The information we need to capture about a task is the name and description. We need to add this as a model to our ToDoList module. Add the task model. It should look similar to this:

```
/* the task */
var task = {
  name: ko.observable(),
  description: ko.observable()
};
```

Chapter 2

We need to capture the tasks in an array. Add the tasks array to the module. It should look similar to this:

```
/* array of tasks */
var tasks = ko.observableArray();
```

 Observable array is an observable, which holds a JavaScript array object as the underlying data structure. You can retrieve the JavaScript array object by invoking the observable array as a function, similar to normal observables.

Now that we have defined our model, let's create an add task method in our module. This method should create a new task, based on the name and description from the task object, and add it to our `tasks` array. We will call our `addTask` method. Create the `addTask` method and add the following line of code:

```
tasks.push({name: task.name(), description: task.description()});
```

The preceding line of code will create a new task and add it to the end of our tasks array. Don't forget to also add code to display the new task on the console. This will help us debug if our code is not working.

 You can use the `unshift` method of the observable array to insert an item to the beginning of the array.

With the model and behavior method defined, we need to expose them publicly so that they can be used from our view. To do this, add these lines of code to the `return` statement of the module. Your `return` statement should look similar to this:

```
return {
  /* add members that will be exposed publicly */
  tasks: tasks,
  task: task,
  addTask: addTask
};
```

One last thing before we start on the view is to activate Knockout. Call the `applyBindings` method of Knockout in the `init` method of our module:

```
var init = function () {
  /* add code to initialize this module */
  ko.applyBindings(ToDoList);
};
```

The init method gets executed when the DOM is ready. This is because we pass the init method to jQuery with the $(init); call.

Now that our module is now ready, let's start on our view. The first step is to capture the user input. We do this by using two HTML inputs: one for the name of the task and another for the description. The HTML inputs are bound to our model by the data-bind construct. We also add a button with the add label. The click of the button is bound to our addTask method. The HTML should look similar to this:

```
<div class="row">
  <div class="col-md-12">
    Name <input type="text" data-bind="value:
    ToDoList.task.name" />
    Description <input type="text" data-bind="value:
    ToDoList.task.description" />
    <button class="btn btn-primary" data-bind="click:
    ToDoList.addTask">Add</button>
  </div>
</div>
```

Try running the application in your browser. You should be able to add a task and see the newly created task in the console. Add code to clear the inputs once the new task is added to the tasks array. This is done by clearing the values of name and description observables from the task object. Do this by creating a clearTask method and calling it from the addTask method after the new task is pushed to the tasks array. Your clearTask method should look similar to this:

```
/* method to clear the task */
var clearTask = function () {
  task.name(null);
  task.description(null);
};
```

Let's now start on the second part of this feature, that is, to view the list of task. We will use the HTML table and foreach binding. Add the following code to the view after the code to capture the inputs and the add button:

```
<table class="table">
  <thead>
    <tr>
      <th>Name</th>
      <th>Description</th>
    </tr>
  </thead>
  <tbody data-bind="foreach: ToDoList.tasks">
    <tr>
```

```
        <td data-bind="text: name"></td>
        <td data-bind="text: description"></td>
      </tr>
    </tbody>
  </table>
```

We have implemented the first feature of our to-do list application. Open the application in the browser and try adding some tasks. It should look similar to this:

We have reached our first checkpoint. The code for this checkpoint can be found at `chapter2\checkpoint1`.

Deleting a task

The second feature of our to-do application is to give the users the ability to delete a task. We will do this by adding an `Actions` column to our tasks table and providing a `Delete` button for each task in the `Actions` column. The task will be removed from the tasks array when the `Delete` button for that task is clicked upon.

Add the `Actions` column to the tasks table by adding the column header to the `thead` element:

```
<th>Actions</th>
```

Add this code after `<th>Description</th>`. Now add the column body with a button for deleting the task. The new column goes after the `Description` column. It should look similar to the following code:

```
<td><button class="btn btn-danger" data-bind="click:
ToDoList.deleteTask">Delete</button></td>
```

The preceding code renders a button with the label, `Delete`, for each of the tasks in our tasks table. The click of the buttons are bound to the `deleteTask` method in our `ToDoList` module.

Let's now add the `deleteTask` method to our module. This method takes a task as a parameter and removes it from the tasks list. We will use the `remove` method of the tasks observable array to remove the specified task. An important point to note is that Knockout automatically passes the current task as the first parameter to our `deleteTask` method. Your `deleteTask` method should look similar to this:

```
/* method to delete task to tasks array */
var deleteTask = function (task) {
  console.log("Deleting task with name: " + task.name);
  //remove the task from the tasks array
  tasks.remove(task);
};
```

Note how we accessed the `name` attribute of the task when we displayed the name of the task in the console. Our tasks in the `tasks` observable array are not observables, so we cannot access the `name` attribute like `task.name()`.

Don't forget to add the `deleteTask` method to the `return` statement of the `ToDoList` module. At this stage, your `return` statement of the module should look similar to this:

```
return {
  /* add members that will be exposed publicly */
  tasks: tasks,
  task: task,
  addTask: addTask,
  deleteTask: deleteTask
};
```

We have implemented the second feature of our to-do list application that gives our users the ability to delete a task. Open the application in the browser and try adding some tasks and then deleting them. It should look similar to this:

We have reached our second checkpoint. The code for this checkpoint can be found at `chapter2\checkpoint2`.

Completing a task

The third feature of our to-do application is to give the users the ability to complete a task. We will do this by adding a `Complete` button for each task in the `Actions` column we created while implementing the delete task feature. The task will be marked as complete by highlighting the row of the tasks that are complete. The `Complete` button will not appear for the tasks that have been completed.

Let's start by adding a new attribute to the task in our `tasks` array that tracks whether the task is complete or not. We will call this attribute, `status`. The status will be set to `new` for the newly created tasks and `complete` for the completed tasks. Add the `status` attribute to the task we create and push to the `tasks` array. The code should look similar to this:

```
//add the task to the tasks array
tasks.push({
  name: task.name(),
  description: task.description(),
  status: 'new'
});
```

Now let's add a button to our `Actions` column to change the status of a task to complete. This button goes above our `Delete` button. This click of the button binds to `completeTask` method in our module:

```
<button class="btn btn-success" data-bind="click:
ToDoList.completeTask">Complete</button>
```

Add the `completeTask` method to the module. Don't forget to add the method to the `return` statement of the module. Knockout will automatically pass the task as the first parameter to our `completeTask` method for which the `Complete` button is clicked upon. The code should look similar to this:

```
/* method to complete a task */
var completeTask = function (task) {
  console.log("Completing task with name: " + task.name);
  //set status of task to complete
  task.status = 'complete';
};
```

Try running the application. You should now see the button with label **Complete** in the **Actions** column alongside the **Delete** button. Try adding and completing some tasks. You should be able to see the status of the tasks changing in the console logs.

The feature in its current state is not very useful to the user as they have no way of knowing the status of the tasks unless, of course, if they open the console window. Let's solve this by highlighting the row of completed task. To achieve this, we will use the `css` data binding on the tasks table row. We will also need to convert our `status` attribute to an observable. We need to do this as we want our view to automatically update when we change the status of a task. To do this, modify the definition of `status` attribute to make it an observable like this:

```
//add the task to the tasks array
tasks.push({
  name: task.name(),
  description: task.description(),
  status: ko.observable('new')
});
```

Modify the `completeTask` method to use the `status` observable. The code that sets the status of the task in the `completeTask` method should now look similar to this:

```
//set status of task to complete
task.status('complete');
```

We are now ready to use the `css` data binding to highlight the row of completed tasks. Add the `css` data bind to the table row like this:

```
<tr data-bind="css: { success: status() == 'complete' }">
```

In the preceding code, `success` is the name of the `css` class to apply to the table row, followed by the condition that specifies when the `css` class should be applied. Knockout will apply the `css` class `success` if the status of the task is `Complete`. Try running the application after making the preceding changes. Add some tasks and try completing them. You should now see the completed tasks highlighted.

One last requirement before we consider this feature complete is to hide the `Complete` button for the tasks that are complete. It does not make sense to complete a task that is already complete. To achieve this, we will use the visible data binding on the `Complete` button. The syntax is similar to the `css` data binding we used on the table row. Modify the `Complete` button to add the visible binding. Your code for the `Complete` button should look similar to this:

```
<button class="btn btn-success" data-bind="visible: status() !=
'complete', click: ToDoList.completeTask">Complete</button>
```

Note that we have multiple bindings on the complete button—the `visible` binding, which is used to only show the button if the status of the task is not complete, and a `click` binding, which binds the click of the button to our `completeTask` method.

> You can restrict the options for task status by using an object instead of using strings, for example:
>
> ```
> var states = {
>     NEW: 'new',
>     COMPLETE: 'complete'
> };
> ```
>
> This will make the code more readable and maintainable.

We have implemented the third feature of our to-do list application that gives our users the ability to complete a task. Open the application in the browser, and try adding some tasks and then completing them. It should look similar to the following:

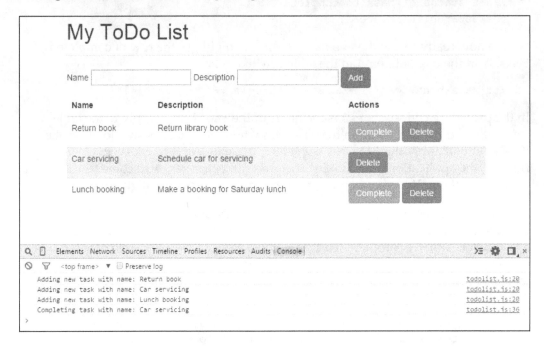

We have reached our third checkpoint. The code for this checkpoint can be found at `chapter2\checkpoint3`.

Setting priority for a task

The fourth feature of our to-do application is to give the users the ability to set priority for tasks. We will do this by adding a dropdown with options for priority. The user will be able to select the appropriate priority when creating a task. The priority of the task will be displayed in a new column in our tasks table. The options for the priority will be 1, 2, and 3.

Let's start by adding the `priority` attribute to our task model. Open the `ToDoList` module in the `todolist.js` file and add the attribute to capture the priority of the task. This attribute must be an observable for two-way data binding to work. Your task model should look similar to this:

```
/* the task */
var task =    {
        name: ko.observable(),
        description: ko.observable(),
        priority: ko.observable()
      };
```

We also need to add this attribute to the task object we create and push to the `tasks` array in our `addTask` method. The `priority` attribute in the task object we create for the `tasks` array does not need to be an observable unless we have a requirement of dynamically updating the view if the priority of the task changes:

```
//add the task to the tasks array
tasks.push({
        name: task.name(),
        description: task.description(),
        priority: task.priority(),
        status: ko.observable('new')
      });
```

We also update our `clearTask` method to include the newly created attribute to capture priority. Give the priority a value of `"1"` as the default priority:

```
/* method to clear the task */
var clearTask = function () {
  task.name(null);
  task.description(null);
  task.priority("1");
};
```

Now that we have modified our module, let's modify the view to capture the task priority. We will use the HTML select element to add the dropdown for our priority options. The code for the priority dropdown looks similar to this:

```
Priority <select data-bind="value: ToDoList.task.priority">
        <option value="1">1</option>
        <option value="2">2</option>
        <option value="3">3</option>
      </select>
```

We bind the value of this `select` element to the `priority` attribute in our task model by using the value data binding, similar to the other input elements.

The next step is to modify the tasks table to add a column for task priority. Add a header column to the tasks table and give it a label. The table header element should look similar to this:

```
<th>Priority</th>
```

Add a column to the tasks table to display the task priority. This column should use the text data binding to display the task priority. It should look similar to this:

```
<td data-bind="text: priority"></td>
```

We have implemented the fourth feature of our to-do list application that gives our users the ability to set the priority for tasks. Open the application in the browser and try adding some tasks with different priorities. It should look similar to the following:

We have reached our fourth checkpoint. The code for this checkpoint can be found at `chapter2\checkpoint4`.

Sorting tasks by priority and name

The fifth feature of our to-do application is to give users the ability to sort our list of tasks by priority and name. We will do this by adding the buttons, which will sort the tasks when clicked upon. This feature will demonstrate the built-in sort function of Knockout.

We will use the `sort` function of the observable array to sort our tasks. The following is the simplest example of using the `sort` function:

```
observableArray.sort();
```

This will sort `observableArray` alphabetically. This simple `sort` function is ideal for arrays of strings or numbers, but for an array of objects, such as our `tasks` array, we need to tell the `sort` function how it should compare objects. To do this, we pass a function to the `sort` function that accepts two objects and returns either a 0, 1, or -1. It should return a 0 if the two objects are equal, 1 if the second object is smaller, and -1 if the first object is smaller. Here is an example which sorts an array of person object by their `firstName`:

```
persons.sort(
  function(left, right) {
      return left.firstName == right.firstName ?
        0
        :
        (left.firstName < right.firstName ? -1 : 1)
  }
);
```

Let's add the sort feature to our to-do list application by first adding methods to our `ToDoList` module that will sort our `tasks` array by priority and name. We will need two methods—a method to sort by priority and another to sort by name. To do this, open the `ToDoList` module in the `todolist.js` file and add a method called `sortByPriority`. In the body of this method, try sorting the tasks array by priority. This should be similar to the preceding example, which sorts an array of persons by their `firstName`. Your `sortByPriority` method should look similar to this:

```
/* method to sort the tasks by priority */
var sortByPriority = function () {
console.log("Sorting tasks by priority");
  tasks.sort(
    function(left, right) {
      return left.priority == right.priority ?
        0
```

Viewing the number of total and completed tasks

The sixth feature of our to-do application is to give the users the ability to view the number of total and completed tasks. We will do this by displaying this information after the tasks table. We will let the user know if no tasks exist in the task list, otherwise, we will display the number of total and competed tasks. This feature will demonstrate the built-in array methods, utility methods provided by Knockout, and computed observables.

Let's get started by displaying the total number of tasks in our `tasks` list. We can use the length property of the observable array to get the number of items it holds. We can access the length property of our tasks array like this:

```
ToDoList.tasks().length;
```

We can display the total number of tasks in our view by using the preceding code. To do this, add a row below the tasks table. Then, use the text data binding with a span element to display the total number of tasks. Your code should look similar to this:

```
<div class="row">
  <div class="col-md-12">
    <strong>
      Total:
        <span data-bind="text:ToDoList.tasks().length">
        </span>
    </strong>
  </div>
</div>
```

We want to display the number of tasks only if the tasks exist in our tasks list, otherwise, we want to display a message letting the users know that no tasks currently exist in the list. Let's do this by using the `visible` binding. Modify the preceding code to add a span element with a `visible` binding. The `visible` binding should only display the element if the length of the tasks array is greater than zero.

Add another span with a `visible` binding to display the element only if the `tasks` array is empty. Add a message to this element to let the user know that no tasks exist in the `tasks` array. Your code should look similar to this:

```
<div class="row">
  <div class="col-md-12">
    <span data-bind="visible: ToDoList.tasks().length > 0">
      <strong>Total: <span data-bind="text: ToDoList.tasks().
      length"></span> </strong>
```

```
    </span>
    <span data-bind="visible: ToDoList.tasks().length == 0">
      <strong>No tasks in my list</strong>
    </span>
  </div>
</div>
```

Open the application in a browser. You should see the message, **No tasks in my list**. Try adding some tasks. The message should now say what the total number of tasks in your list is.

The first part of this feature was not that hard to implement. It did not require any changes to our ToDoList module. In the second part of this feature, we will display the number of completed tasks. For this we will use computed observable and a method from the Knockout utilities to filter our tasks array.

 Knockout provides a number of useful methods in ko.utils package. These methods range from manipulating arrays to handling JSON data.

Let's first create a skeleton for our computed observable that will return the number of completed tasks. Call the computed observable, numOfCompletedTasks. This computed observable will depend on the tasks observable array and its value will be updated by Knockout every time the tasks observable array is updated. The skeleton of numOfCompletedTasks should look similar to this:

```
/* observable to compute number of completed tasks */
var numOfCompletedTasks = ko.computed(function() {
  //add code to return number of completed tasks
});
```

You can loop through the tasks array and count the number of completed tasks or use the arrayFilter method of the ko.utils package. The arrayFilter method returns an array, which contains items specified by a matching criteria. The criteria is passing as a function to arrayFilter. The criteria in our case is that the status of the task should be 'complete'. Let's write code to get an array of completed tasks by using the arrayFilter method of ko.utils. Once you have the array of completed tasks, its length property can be returned by the numOfCompletedTasks computed observable. Your numOfCompletedTasks computed observable should look similar to this:

```
/* observable to compute number of completed tasks */
var numOfCompletedTasks = ko.computed(function() {
  var completedTasks = ko.utils.arrayFilter(tasks(),
  function(task) {
```

```
        return task.status() == 'complete';
    });
    return completedTasks.length;
});
```

Add the `numOfCompletedTasks` computed observable to the `return` statement of the module so that it can be used by our view. Next, we need to update our view to use the newly created computed observable. Update the view to use the computed observable with a text binding, similar to the binding to display the total number of tasks. To do this, add this line inside the `span` element, which gets displayed when the `tasks` array has tasks. The code should look similar to this:

```
<span data-bind="visible: ToDoList.tasks().length > 0">
<strong>Total: <span data-bind="text:
ToDoList.tasks().length"></span>
</strong>
<strong>Completed: <span data-bind="text: ToDoList.
numOfCompletedTasks()"></span>
</strong>
</span>
```

We have implemented the sixth feature of our to-do list application that gives our users the ability to view the number of total and completed tasks. Open the application in the browser and add some tasks. Try completing some tasks and view the number of total and completed tasks change. In the browser, it should look similar to this:

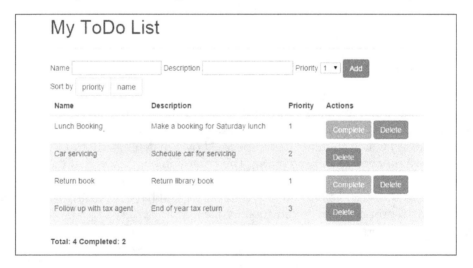

We have reached our fifth checkpoint. The code for this checkpoint can be found at `chapter2\checkpoint6`.

 Try using `ko.pureComputed` instead of `ko.computed` for `numOfCompletedTasks`. It is better to use `ko.pureComputed` if the computed observable simply returns a value and does not change the state of any object. The `ko.pureComputed` function prevents memory leaks and reduces computation overheads.

Summary

In this chapter, we built a to-do list application. The application allowed the user to create and manage tasks. The features included adding, viewing, deleting, sorting, and completing tasks. It also included features to set the priority on tasks and viewing the number of total and completed tasks.

We started with building a feature for adding and viewing tasks. This feature built on the concepts learned in the previous chapter. The features demonstrated the use of value and click binding to bind input components such as text fields and buttons. It also demonstrated the use of `foreach` binding to render the tasks in a table.

The second feature we built was to delete a task from the tasks list. This feature enhanced the concepts of working with `observable` arrays and demonstrated how to remove an item from an array. The third feature was to complete a task. In building this feature, we learned how to modify an item in the `observable` array. We also learned the use of `css` binding to control the appearance of components and visible binding to show or hide components. The fourth feature was to set a priority of a task. This feature reinforced the concepts of value and text bindings. The fifth feature was to sort our tasks list by priority and name. In building this feature, we learned the use of the `sort` method provided by the `observable` array.

The last feature we built was to display the number of total and completed tasks. The two most important concepts we learned were the use of computed `observable` and `ko.utils` package.

In the next chapter, we will learn how to develop a rich and dynamic form to capture user information.

3
Creating an Online Customer Registration Form

Forms are used to capture and submit user input in most web-based applications. One common example is a customer registration form. This chapter will walk you through building a dynamic customer registration form application. You will learn the controls Knockout provides to help build a dynamic and rich form easily and efficiently.

In this chapter, you will learn how to:

- Work with form fields
- Bind different form elements with the Knockout model
- Show or hide form elements based on business logic
- Dynamically create form elements and bind them to a list
- Submit the form using the submit data binding

The online customer registration form allows the user to provide the information required for user registration. The application has the following features:

- Capture personal information that includes customer's title and name
- Capture customer's contact details that includes e-mail address and phone numbers
- Capture customer's residential and postal address
- Capture credit card details for payments
- Capture customer's interests
- Clear the registration form

Getting started

The first thing to do is to create the skeleton for our customer registration form application. You should be familiar with these steps from the previous chapter.

Create the folder structure for development by following these steps:

1. Create the folder RegistrationForm. This is the main folder that houses our customer registration form application.
2. Add a WebContent folder under the RegistrationForm folder. This folder holds the content that gets published to the web.
3. Add a javascript folder under the WebContent folder. As the folder name suggests, this folder will contain all our JavaScript files.
4. Add a bootstrap folder under the WebContent folder. This folder will contain the Bootstrap files.

Now that we have the folder structure in place, let's add the files to our folders by following these steps:

1. Add the Knockout library to the javascript folder.
2. Add the jQuery library to the javascript folder.
3. Add Bootstrap to the bootstrap folder.
4. Create the registrationform.js file under the javascript folder.
5. Create the registrationform.html file under the WebContent folder.

Following the preceding steps should result in a folder structure similar to this:

Now that we have created the folder structure, we can add code to our HTML and JavaScript files. Open the `registrationform.html` file and add the following HTML code:

```
<!DOCTYPE HTML>
<html>
  <head>
    <meta http-equiv="Content-Type" content="text/html" />
    <title>Knockout : Registration Form Example</title>

    <link rel="stylesheet" href="bootstrap/css/bootstrap.min.css">

    <script type="text/javascript"
    src="javascript/jquery-2.1.3.min.js"></script>
    <script type="text/javascript"
    src="javascript/knockout-3.2.0.js"></script>
    <script type="text/javascript"
    src="bootstrap/js/bootstrap.min.js"></script>
    <script type="text/javascript"
    src="javascript/registrationform.js"></script>
  </head>
  <body>
    <div class="container">
      <div class="page-header">
        <h1>Registration Form</h1>
      </div>
      <!-- Registration form goes here -->
    </div>
  </body>
</html>
```

The preceding code references the required libraries and displays a page header with the name of our application. Open the `registrationform.js` file and add the following code; the code defines our empty `RegistrationForm` module:

```
/* Module for Registration form application */
var RegistrationForm = function () {
  /* add members here */

  var init = function () {
    /* add code to initialize this module */
    ko.applyBindings(RegistrationForm);
  };

  /* execute the init function when the DOM is ready */
```

```
    $(init);

    return {
       /* add members that will be exposed publicly */
    };
}();
```

View the application in the browser. It should give you a page with the page header. We are now ready to add a form to our skeleton.

We will use the HTML form element with the Knockout submit data binding to build our customer registration form. The submit binding is typically only used with the HTML form element. Using the submit binding, you specify the method that should be called when the form is submitted.

 The submit binding will prevent the default submit action of the form and instead, it will call the method you specify. You can return a true from your specified method if you want the default submit action to be executed.

Let's add a form element to our HTML with the submit data binding by adding the following code under the page header:

```
<form data-bind="submit: RegistrationForm.submit">
   <button type="Submit" class="btn btn-primary">Submit</button>
</form>
```

The preceding code has our HTML form with a submit data binding. The submit binding specifies that a method called submit in our RegistrationForm module should be called when the form is submitted. The form also has a Submit button. Clicking on the Submit button submits the form causing our submit method to be called. Let's add the submit method to our RegistrationForm module. Update the RegistrationForm module and add the submit method. The submit method also needs to be added to the module's return statement. The method should look similar to this:

```
/* form submission */
var submit = function () {
   console.log("The form is submitted");
};
```

Open the application in your browser. You should see a page with the application header and a submit button. Try clicking the submit button and view the output in the console window.

Now that we have the basic skeleton with form in place, let's get started and build the first feature of our customer registration form application.

Capturing personal information

The first feature of our customer registration form application is to capture the title and first, middle, and last name of the customer. We will use a drop-down input component to capture the title. The name fields will be captured using the input text fields. The information will be captured in a model.

Let's start with the names fields as they are simple to implement. Add a model to the `RegistrationForm` module to capture the customer's first, middle, and last names. The attributes of the model must be Knockout observables for a two-way binding between the model and the view. We will call our model `customer` and add an attribute to group personal information. The model should look similar to this:

```
/* the model */
var customer = {
  personalInfo: {
    firstName: ko.observable(),
    middleName: ko.observable(),
    lastName: ko.observable()
  }
};
```

Add the model to the `return` statement of the module to make it accessible from the view. Now we can add the name input fields to the view and bind them to the model. Open the view in `registrationform.html`. Add a `fieldset` element as a child of the form element before the `Submit` button. We use the `fieldset` element to group a set of related form elements, in our case, the personal information fields. Add a heading to the `fieldset` element for personal information.

> Use the grid system provided by Bootstrap to layout your form. This will give you a responsive layout, which appropriately scales up as the device size increases. You can find more on Bootstrap grid system at `http://getbootstrap.com/css/#grid`.

Now add input elements and their corresponding labels to capture the name fields. Bind the input elements to their corresponding attributes in the model by using the value data binding, similar to the examples in the previous chapters, using the `input` elements and `value` data binding. Use the Bootstrap grid system to give your form an appropriate layout. My `fieldset` looks similar to this:

```
<fieldset>
  <div class="row">
    <div class="col-md-12">
      <h4>Personal Information</h4>
    </div>
  </div>
  <div class="row">
    <div class="col-md-4">
      <div class="form-group">
        <label for="firstNameInput">First Name</label>
        <input type="text" class="form-control" data-bind="value:
        RegistrationForm.customer.personalInfo.firstName"
        id="firstNameInput" placeholder="Enter first name">
      </div>
    </div>
    <div class="col-md-4">
      <div class="form-group">
        <label for="middleNameInput">Middle Name</label>
        <input type="text" class="form-control" data-bind="value:
        RegistrationForm.customer.personalInfo.middleName"
        id="middleNameInput" placeholder="Enter middle name">
      </div>
    </div>
    <div class="col-md-4">
      <div class="form-group">
        <label for="lastNameInput">Last Name</label>
        <input type="text" class="form-control" data-bind="value:
        RegistrationForm.customer.personalInfo.lastName"
        id="lastNameInput" placeholder="Enter last name">
      </div>
    </div>
  </div>
</fieldset>
```

The preceding code displays a header using the h4 element, which describes the set of input fields; in this case, it is Personal Information. This is followed by a set of label and input elements grouped by a div element with the form-group class. The input fields are bound to the corresponding attributes in the model by using the value data binding. The header and the form fields are laid out using the BootStrap grid system.

 Knockout provides a helper method, ko.toJSON, which returns a JSON string representation of the model.

Update the submit method in the RegistrationForm module to display the contents of the model in the console. This can be done by adding the following code to the submit method:

```
console.log(ko.toJSON(customer));
```

View registrationform.html in the browser. Make sure that you have the console window of the browser open. You should see the name fields with their labels. Try entering information in the input fields and hit the **Submit** button. You should see the data appear in the console window.

The next step is to add a drop-down field to capture the customer's title. In the previous chapter, we used the HTML select element as a drop-down field to capture task priority. We could use the select element to capture a customer's title, however, Bootstrap advises against using the select element as it cannot be fully styled in some browser. Instead, it recommends and provides a drop-down component. This component is a div element with a class "dropdown". The div element has two subcomponents, a button and an unordered list. The button represents the unexpanded dropdown and the selected value as its text. The unordered list represents the options for the dropdown.

 Avoid using HTML select element with Bootstrap as it cannot be fully styled in some browsers. Use the dropdown component provided by Bootstrap. You can find out more about Bootstrap dropdown at http://getbootstrap.com/components/#dropdowns.

We will use the Bootstrap dropdown component to capture the customer's title. To use this component, we need the Bootstrap JavaScript plugin, which is provided by Bootstrap. Add the following line of code in the HTML header before the registrationform.js to include this plugin. The HTML header should look similar to this:

```
<head>
  <meta http-equiv="Content-Type" content="text/html" />
  <title>Knockout : Registration Form Example</title>
  <link rel="stylesheet" href="bootstrap/css/bootstrap.min.css">
  <script type="text/javascript"
  src="javascript/jquery-2.1.3.min.js"></script>
  <script type="text/javascript"
  src="javascript/knockout-3.2.0.js"></script>
  <script type="text/javascript"
  src="bootstrap/js/bootstrap.min.js"></script>
  <script type="text/javascript"
  src="javascript/registrationform.js"></script>
</head>
```

The Bootstrap dropdown component contains multiple elements and hence, we cannot use a single binding to bind this component to our model. We will bind individual components in the dropdown and also develop a custom two-way binding. Let's start by adding the title attribute to our model. The model should now look similar to this:

```
/* the model */
var customer = {
  personalInfo: {
    title: ko.observable(),
    firstName: ko.observable(),
    middleName: ko.observable(),
    lastName: ko.observable()
  }
};
```

Now, let's add the dropdown component to our view with its label:

```
<div class="form-group">
  <label for="titleInput">Title</label>
  <div class="dropdown">
    <button class="btn btn-default dropdown-toggle" type="button"
    id="titleInput" data-toggle="dropdown" aria-expanded="true" >
      select
      <span class="caret"></span>
    </button>
```

```
  <ul class="dropdown-menu" role="menu"
  aria-labelledby="titleInput">
    <li role="presentation"><a role="menuitem"
    tabindex="-1">Mr</a></li>
    <li role="presentation"><a role="menuitem"
    tabindex="-1">Mrs</a></li>
    <li role="presentation"><a role="menuitem"
    tabindex="-1">Miss</a></li>
    <li role="presentation"><a role="menuitem"
    tabindex="-1">Dr</a></li>
  </ul>
 </div>
</div>
```

The preceding code will add a dropdown with a value of select and options for the different titles. The options in the dropdown use the anchor element. We need to capture the click of the anchor element and update our model accordingly. To do this, we will use the click data binding. We can also make the options list dynamic by using the foreach data binding on the ul element. To do this, modify the RegistrationForm module to add an array for title options. The items in the array should also include a method to update the model with the value of the option when the anchor is clicked upon. The array should look similar to this:

```
/* options for the title drop down*/
var titleOptions = [
  {
    value: 'Mr',
    setTitle: function () {
    RegistrationForm.customer.personalInfo.title("Mr"); }
  },
  {
    value: 'Mrs',
    setTitle: function () {
    RegistrationForm.customer.personalInfo.title("Mrs");}
  },
  {
    value: 'Miss',
    setTitle: function () {
    RegistrationForm.customer.personalInfo.title("Miss");}
  },
  {
    value: 'Dr',
    setTitle: function () {
    RegistrationForm.customer.personalInfo.title("Dr");}
  }
];
```

The array contains objects with two attributes: a `value` attribute that specifies the value of the option and a `setTitle` attribute, which is a method to update the customer model with the value of the option. Add this array to the `return` statement of the module.

Let's now modify the view to use this new array. Modify the `ul` element to use the options array from our model. It should look similar to this:

```
<ul class="dropdown-menu" role="menu" aria-labelledby="titleInput"
data-bind="foreach: RegistrationForm.titleOptions">
  <li role="presentation"><a role="menuitem" tabindex="-1"
  data-bind="text: value, click: setTitle"></a></li>
</ul>
```

The preceding code uses the `foreach` binding on the `ul` element to render the options list. Each list element uses a text binding for the text to be displayed and a click binding to specify the method to be called when the element is clicked upon.

Try running the application with the preceding modification. You should be able to see the value of the title attribute change in the model when the form is submitted. You will notice that although the model gets updated with the value of the title selected, the drop-down label still says select. This can be fixed by using computed observable to update the text of the button in the dropdown to the selected value of the title. We will use the pure computed observable as the computed observable is not changing any attribute in our model. Write a pure computed observable to return the value of title from our model. This computed observable should return `"select"` if the title is not set. Add the code to the `RegistrationForm` module and update the `return` statement to return this method:

```
/* computed observable for title drop down text change */
var titleSelect = ko.pureComputed(function () {
  if(customer.personalInfo.title() == null) {
    return "select"
  } else {
    return customer.personalInfo.title();
  }
});
```

Modify the drop-down button in the view to use this computed observable. The button should look similar to this:

```
<button class="btn btn-default dropdown-toggle" type="button"
id="titleInput" data-toggle="dropdown" aria-expanded="true" >
  <span data-bind="text: RegistrationForm.titleSelect"> </span>
  <span class="caret"></span>
</button>
```

The button uses a span element with a text binding to display the title in the dropdown.

We have implemented the first feature of our customer registration form application. Open the application in the browser. Try selecting the customer's title from the dropdown and entering the name fields. Click on **Submit** to see the data entered appear in the console window. It should look similar to this:

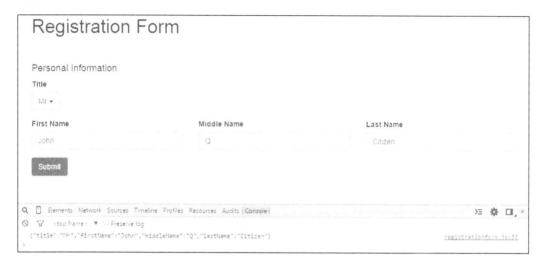

We have reached our first checkpoint. The code for this checkpoint can be found at chapter3\checkpoint1.

Capturing contact details

The second feature of our customer registration form application is to capture the customers contact details. We will capture the phone number and e-mail address of the customer. We will also ask for the customer's preferred contact. The phone number and the e-mail will be captured using input text fields and the preferred contact will be captured using radio buttons.

Let's start by adding attributes for the phone number and e-mail fields to our customer model. Add an attribute to group the fields; we will call it `contactDetails`. Now add the attributes for phone number and e-mail under `contactDetails`. Our model should now look similar to this:

```
/* the model */
var customer = {
  personalInfo: {
    title: ko.observable(),
    firstName: ko.observable(),
    middleName: ko.observable(),
    lastName: ko.observable()
  },
  contactDetails: {
    phoneNumber: ko.observable(),
    emailAddress: ko.observable(),
    preferredContact: ko.observable()
  }
};
```

The next step is to update the view to add the new fields. We start by adding a `fieldset` for the contact details. The `fieldset` should contain the section header and a `div` row that will contain the `div` element for our input fields. Now add the input fields for the phone number and e-mail address. Bind the input fields to the model in our `RegistrationForm`, similar to the fields for personal information. The `fieldset` for contact details should look similar to this:

```
<fieldset>
  <div class="row">
    <div class="col-md-12">
      <h4>Contact Details</h4>
    </div>
  </div>
  <div class="row">
    <div class="col-md-4">
      <div class="form-group">
        <label for="phoneNumberInput">Phone Number</label>
        <input type="text" class="form-control" data-bind="value:
        RegistrationForm.customer.contactDetails.phoneNumber"
        id="phoneNumberInput" placeholder="Enter phone number">
      </div>
    </div>
    <div class="col-md-4">
      <div class="form-group">
        <label for="emailAddressInput">Email</label>
```

```
         <input type="text" class="form-control" data-bind="value:
         RegistrationForm.customer.contactDetails.emailAddress"
         id="emailAddressInput" placeholder="Enter email address">
      </div>
    </div>
  </div>
</fieldset>
```

Try running the application in your browser. You should be able to see the phone number and e-mail address fields. Enter information in the fields and hit **Submit**. Data entered in the fields should appear in the console logs.

Let's start with the second part of this feature that is to capture the preferred contact of our customer. The preferred contacts will be captured using radio buttons. We will have one radio button for each contact type — one for email address and another for phone number. We already created the attribute in our model for preferred contact. We now have to update our view to add the radio buttons. We will use the checked binding to bind the radio buttons value to our model.

 The checked binding binds form controls that are checkable, such as radio buttons and checkboxes, with attributes in the model.

Add the radio buttons to the view inside the fieldset tag after the inputs for the phone number and e-mail in the contact details. Bind the radio buttons to the model using the checked binding and the Bootstrap grid system for layout, similar to the previous inputs. My code with the radio buttons looks similar to this:

```
<div class="row">
  <div class="col-md-4">
    <label>Preferred Contact</label>
    <div class="form-group">
      <label class="radio-inline">
        <input type="radio" value="phone"
        name="preferredContactInput" data-bind="checked:
        RegistrationForm.customer.contactDetails.
        preferredContact">Phone
      </label>
      <label class="radio-inline">
        <input type="radio" value="email"
        name="preferredContactInput" data-bind="checked:
        RegistrationForm.customer.contactDetails.
        preferredContact">Email
      </label>
    </div>
  </div>
</div>
```

The `checked` binding in the preceding code will set the value of the attribute in the model to the value specified by the `value` attribute of the input. In other words, the `preferredContact` attribute in our model will be set to `phone` when the radio button with the label **Phone** is checked. Another important thing to note is the use of the `name` attribute on the radio button input fields. The value of the `name` attribute is the same for both the input fields to specify that they both belong to the `preferedContactInput` group.

We have implemented the second feature of our customer registration form application. Open the application in the browser. Try selecting the customer's title from the dropdown and entering the name fields. Enter the contact details and select the preferred contact. Click on **Submit** to see the data entered appear in the console window. It should look similar to this:

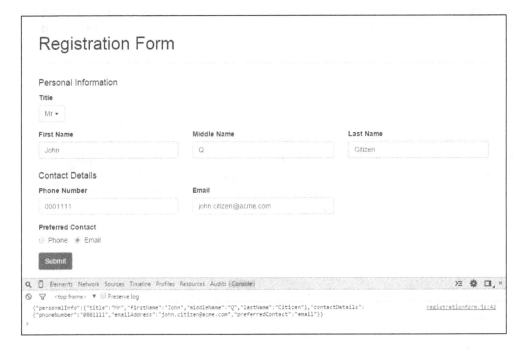

We have reached our second checkpoint. The code for this checkpoint can be found at `chapter3\checkpoint2`.

Capturing residential and postal addresses

The third feature of our customer registration form application is to capture the customer's residential and postal address. For residential address, we will capture the street address, city, post code, and country. For postal address, we will give users a choice between a PO Box and street address. The choice between a PO Box and street address will be captured using radio buttons, and the appropriate fields will be displayed. For PO Box address, we will capture the PO Box, city, post code, and country.

Let's start by creating the `address` attribute in our customer model. The `address` attribute will hold attributes for residential and postal addresses. Create the address and residential attributes. In our customer model, the attributes should look similar to this:

```
address: {
  residential: {
    street: ko.observable(),
    city: ko.observable(),
    postCode: ko.observable(),
    country: ko.observable()
  }
}
```

The next step is to update the view to add the new fields. We start by adding a `fieldset` element for the addresses. This should go after the contact details and before the `Submit` button. The `fieldset` element should contain the section headers and a `div` row that will contain the `div` element for our input fields, similar to the previous examples. Create the `fieldset` and the section headers. It should look similar to this:

```
<fieldset>
  <div class="row">
    <div class="col-md-12">
      <h4>Address Details</h4>
    </div>
  </div>
  <div class="row">
    <div class="col-md-12">
      <h5>Residential Address</h5>
    </div>
  </div>
  <!-- Add input fields here -->
</fieldset>
```

Now add the input fields to capture the residential address. Bind the input fields to their corresponding attributes in the model. Feel free to layout the input fields as appropriate. With the layout, the fields should look similar to this:

```
<div class="form-group">
  <label for="streetInput">Street Address</label>
  <input type="text" class="form-control" data-bind="value:
  RegistrationForm.customer.address.residential.street"
  id="streetInput" placeholder="Enter street address">
</div>
<div class="form-group">
  <label for="cityInput">City</label>
  <input type="text" class="form-control" data-bind="value:
  RegistrationForm.customer.address.residential.city"
  id="cityInput" placeholder="Enter city">
</div>
<div class="form-group">
  <label for="postCodeInput">Postcode</label>
  <input type="text" class="form-control" data-bind="value:
  RegistrationForm.customer.address.residential.postCode"
  id="postCodeInput" placeholder="Enter postcode">
</div>
<div class="form-group">
  <label for="countryInput">Country</label>
  <input type="text" class="form-control" data-bind="value:
  RegistrationForm.customer.address.residential.country"
  id="countryInput" placeholder="Enter country">
</div>
```

Try running the application in your browser. You should be able to see the fields for the residential address. Enter information in the fields and hit **Submit**. Data entered in the fields should appear in the console logs.

Now, we will move to the second part of this feature that is to capture the postal address of the customer. As mentioned earlier, the postal address can be either a street address or a PO Box address. To develop this, we will need to capture the type of postal address in our model. This will be done using radio buttons. We will also need attributes for street and PO Box address. We will create two separate views for postal address — one for street address and another for PO Box address. The appropriate view will be displayed based on the user selection. Update the customer model to add the postal address. The postal address goes in the `address` attribute as it is a part of the address:

```
address: {
  residential: {
    street: ko.observable(),
```

```
      city: ko.observable(),
      postCode: ko.observable(),
      country: ko.observable()
    },
    postal: {
      type: ko.observable(),
      streetAddress: {
        street: ko.observable(),
        city: ko.observable(),
        postCode: ko.observable(),
        country: ko.observable()
      },
      poBoxAddress: {
        poBox:  ko.observable(),
        city: ko.observable(),
        postCode: ko.observable(),
        country: ko.observable()
      }
    }
  }
```

Note that we have added a `type` attribute for the postal address. This attribute will be used to specify whether the postal address is a PO Box or street address. We have also added attributes for street and PO Box addresses.

Now that our model is ready, let's work on the view. The first step is to add a section header and the radio buttons for postal address type. Add the section header for postal address. The section header goes under the section for residential address. Now add the radio buttons—one for street address type and another for PO Box address type. Make sure that both the radio buttons belong to the same group by specifying the same name attribute. Bind the radio buttons to the `type` attribute of the postal address. Give the radio buttons an appropriate value. We will use the value of the radio button later with the visible binding to show or hide address fields. So far, your code for the postal address should look similar to this:

```
<div class="row">
  <div class="col-md-12">
    <h5>Postal Address</h5>
  </div>
</div>
<div class="row">
  <div class="col-md-4">
    <label>Select postal address type</label>
    <div class="form-group">
      <label class="radio-inline">
```

```
      <input type="radio" value="street"
      name="postalAddressTypeInput" data-bind="checked:
      RegistrationForm.customer.address.postal.type">Street
      address
    </label>
    <label class="radio-inline">
      <input type="radio" value="pobox"
      name="postalAddressTypeInput" data-bind="checked:
      RegistrationForm.customer.address.postal.type">PO Box
    </label>
  </div>
</div>
</div>
```

The next step is to add sections for street and PO Box addresses. Add two sections to the `div` elements below the radio buttons — one for street address and another for PO Box address. Add a visible binding to the `div` elements that shows or hides the sections based on the `type` attribute of the postal address form the model. Add a temporary text in the `div` elements, which will later be replaced by the appropriate address fields. Your two `div` elements should look similar to this:

```
<div data-bind="visible:
RegistrationForm.customer.address.postal.type() == 'street'">
  street address
  <!-- add postal street address fields here -->
</div>
<div data-bind="visible:
RegistrationForm.customer.address.postal.type() == 'pobox'">
  PO Box address
  <!-- add postal street address fields here -->
</div>
```

View the application in the browser. You should see the section for postal address and radio button group to select the type of postal address. Try selecting either street or PO Box address. You should see the section for the selected type appear.

It's now time to add the address fields for the street and PO Box address to the view. The fields for street address are similar to the street address for residential. You can copy the fields from residential address. Don't forget to change the IDs and bindings. Add the fields to the section for street address. This section will look similar to this:

```
<div data-bind="visible:
RegistrationForm.customer.address.postal.type() == 'street'">
  <div class="row">
```

```
    <div class="col-md-12">
      <div class="form-group">
        <label for="postalStreetInput">Street Address</label>
        <input type="text" class="form-control" data-bind="value:
        RegistrationForm.customer.address.postal.streetAddress.street"
        id="postalStreetInput"
        placeholder="Enter street address">
      </div>
    </div>
  </div>
  <div class="row">
    <div class="col-md-5">
      <div class="form-group">
        <label for="postalCityInput">City</label>
        <input type="text" class="form-control" data-bind="value:
        RegistrationForm.customer.address.postal.streetAddress.city"
        id="postalCityInput" placeholder="Enter city">
      </div>
    </div>
    <div class="col-md-2">
      <div class="form-group">
        <label for="postalPostCodeInput">Postcode</label>
        <input type="text" class="form-control" data-bind="value:
        RegistrationForm.customer.address.postal.streetAddress.
        postCode" id="postalPostCodeInput"
        placeholder="Enter postcode">
      </div>
    </div>
    <div class="col-md-5">
      <div class="form-group">
        <label for="postalCountryInput">Country</label>
        <input type="text" class="form-control"
        data-bind="value:
        RegistrationForm.customer.address.postal.streetAddress.
        country"
        id="postalCountryInput" placeholder="Enter country">
      </div>
    </div>
  </div>
</div>
```

Add the fields for the PO Box address in the PO Box address section and bind them to the corresponding attributes in the model. The fields of the PO Box address are PO Box, city, postcode, and country. The PO Box address section should look similar to this:

```
<div data-bind="visible:
RegistrationForm.customer.address.postal.type() == 'pobox'">
  <div class="row">
    <div class="col-md-12">
      <div class="form-group">
        <label for="poBoxInput">PO Box</label>
        <input type="text" class="form-control"
        data-bind="value:
        RegistrationForm.customer.address.postal.poBoxAddress.poBox"
        id="poBoxInput" placeholder="Enter PO Box">
      </div>
    </div>
  </div>
  <div class="row">
    <div class="col-md-5">
      <div class="form-group">
        <label for="poBoxCityInput">City</label>
        <input type="text" class="form-control" data-bind="value:
        RegistrationForm.customer.address.postal.poBoxAddress.city"
        id="poBoxCityInput" placeholder="Enter city">
      </div>
    </div>
    <div class="col-md-2">
      <div class="form-group">
        <label for="poBoxPostCodeInput">Postcode</label>
        <input type="text" class="form-control"
        data-bind="value:
        data-bind="value:
        RegistrationForm.customer.address.postal.poBoxAddress.
        postCode" id="poBoxPostCodeInput"
        placeholder="Enter postcode">
      </div>
    </div>
    <div class="col-md-5">
      <div class="form-group">
        <label for="poBoxCountryInput">Country</label>
        <input type="text" class="form-control"
        data-bind="value:
        RegistrationForm.customer.address.postal.poBoxAddress.country"
        id="poBoxCountryInput" placeholder="Enter country">
      </div>
    </div>
  </div>
</div>
```

We have implemented the third feature of our customer registration form application. Open the application in the browser. Try selecting the customer's title from the dropdown and entering the name fields. Enter the contact details and select the preferred contact. Enter details of the customer's address, including residential and postal addresses. Click on **Submit** to see the data entered appear in the console window. The application should look similar to this; the screenshot only shows the address details section:

We have reached our third checkpoint. The code for this checkpoint can be found at `chapter3\checkpoint3`.

Capturing credit card details

The forth feature of our customer registration form application is to capture the customer's credit card details. For the credit card, we will capture the name on the card, card number, and card expiry date. We will let our customer register more than one credit cards and limit it to a maximum of three.

Let's start by creating the credit card attribute in our `customer` model. This attribute will hold the details of the credit cards. This attribute will be an observable array as we need to allow our customers to register multiple credit cards. Add the following code to the `customer` model:

```
creditCards: ko.observableArray()
```

We need to add one credit card to our array initially so that it appears on the view. To do this, we will add a method to our module that will add a credit card and then call it from our `init` method. The add credit card method should look similar to this:

```
/* method to add credit card to the credit cards array */
var addCreditCard = function () {
  customer.creditCards.push({name: ko.observable(), number:
  ko.observable(), expiryDate: ko.observable()});
};
```

This method simply pushes a credit card to the array. The attributes of the credit card are `name`, `number`, and `expiryDate`. The attributes are observables for two-way binding to work. Call this method from the `init` method of the module. This gives us our first credit card when we run the application:

```
var init = function () {
  /* add code to initialize this module */
  //add the first credit card
  addCreditCard();
  //apply ko bindings
  ko.applyBindings(RegistrationForm);
};
```

We can now update our view to add the credit card fields. Add a `fieldset` element and credit card section header, similar to the previous sections. Add a `div` element, which will hold our credit card fields. The section should look similar to this:

```
<fieldset>
  <div class="row">
    <div class="col-md-12">
      <h4>Credit Cards</h4>
    </div>
  </div>
  <div>
  <!-- Add credit card fields here -->
  </div>
</fieldset>
```

We need to traverse the `creditCards` array from our model to render the cards. We will use the `foreach` binding to achieve this. Add the `foreach` binding to the `div` element and then add the input fields to capture the credit card details. Bind the input fields to the corresponding attributes in the model. With the `foreach` binding and the input fields, the `div` element should look similar to this:

```
<div data-bind="foreach: RegistrationForm.customer.creditCards">
  <div class="row">
    <div class="col-md-4">
      <div class="form-group">
        <label for="ccNameInput">Name on card</label>
        <input type="text" class="form-control" data-bind="value:
        name" id="ccNameInput" placeholder="Enter name on card">
      </div>
    </div>
    <div class="col-md-4">
      <div class="form-group">
        <label for="ccNumberInput">Card Number</label>
        <input type="text" class="form-control" data-bind="value:
        number" id="ccNumberInput"
        placeholder="Enter card number">
      </div>
    </div>
    <div class="col-md-2">
      <div class="form-group">
        <label for="ccExpiryDateInput">Card Number</label>
        <input type="text" class="form-control"
        data-bind="value: expiryDate" id="ccExpiryDateInput"
        placeholder="mm/yy">
      </div>
    </div>
  </div>
</div>
```

Try running the application in the browser. You should see the section for credit cards. The section should have a row, containing input fields for one credit card. Try entering the information and click on **Submit**. You should see the credit card details entered appear in the logs.

The next step is to allow the customers to add additional cards. To do this, we will add a link at the bottom of the credit card section and bind its click event to our add credit card method. The link should look similar to this:

```
<a href data-bind="click: RegistrationForm.addCreditCard">+ credit
card</a>
```

Add the `addCreditCard` method to the `return` statement of the module as it is now accessed from the view. Try running the application in the browser and add some credit cards.

We need to limit the credit card to a maximum of three. We will only show the link if the number of credit cards in the list are less than three. To do this, we will use the visible binding on the `div` element surrounding the link. The visible binding will check for the number of items in the observable array. After applying the visible binding to its surrounding `div`, the link looks similar to this:

```
<div class="row" data-bind="visible:
RegistrationForm.customer.creditCards().length < 3">
  <div class="col-md-4">
    <a href data-bind="click: RegistrationForm.addCreditCard">+
    credit card</a>
  </div>
</div>
```

The preceding code checks for the length of our `creditCards` observable array and only displays the `div` element if the length of the array is less than three.

As a final step, we will give our customers the ability to delete a credit card. To do this, we will add a delete link to the row, containing the credit card. Clicking on this link will delete the credit card item from the array. The deleted link will only appear if there is more than one item in our array.

Let's update our view to add the delete link. Bind the delete link to the `deleteCreditCard` method in our module. We will create this method after updating the view. Add visible binding to the `div` surrounding the delete link. Make the link only appear if there are more than one items in the `creditCards` array. The code for the delete link should look similar to this:

```
<div class="col-md-1" data-bind="visible:
RegistrationForm.customer.creditCards().length > 1">
  <div class="form-group">
    <label for="ccActionInput">Action</label>
    <a href id="ccActionInput" data-bind="click:
    RegistrationForm.deleteCreditCard">delete</a>
  </div>
</div>
```

The final step is to add the `deleteCreditCard` method to our module. The method will take the credit card item as its input parameter and remove it from the `creditCards` observable array. Create this method in the module and add it to the `return` statement. The method should look similar to this:

```
/* method to delete a credit card from the credit cards array */
var deleteCreditCard = function (card) {
  console.log("Deleting credit card with number: " +
  card.number());
  //remove the credit card from the array
  customer.creditCards.remove(card);
}
```

We have implemented the fourth feature of our customer registration form application. Open the application in the browser. Try entering credit card information and adding or deleting credit cards. The application should look similar to this; the following screenshot only shows the credit card section:

We have reached our fourth checkpoint. The code for this checkpoint can be found at `chapter3\checkpoint4`.

Capturing interests

The fifth feature of our customer registration form application is to capture the customer's interests. The interest categories are sports, news, movies, and comedy. We will capture the interests using checkboxes.

Let's start by creating the interests attribute in our `customer` model. This attribute will hold the values of the interests selected by the customer. This attribute will be an observable array as we need to allow the customer to select multiple interest categories. Add the following code to the `customer` model:

```
interests: ko.observableArray()
```

We will now update the view to add the checkboxes and bind them to the interests attribute. Add a `fieldset` element and interests section header, similar to the previous sections. Add a `div` element, which will hold our interest checkboxes. Add the interest checkboxes and give them values of the interest categories. Bind the checkboxes to the interests attribute of the model. The interests `fieldset` should look similar to this:

```html
<fieldset>
  <div class="row">
    <div class="col-md-12">
      <h4>Interests</h4>
    </div>
  </div>
  <div class="row">
    <div class="col-md-12">
      <div class="checkbox">
        <label class="checkbox-inline">
          <input type="checkbox" value="sports"
          data-bind="checked:
          RegistrationForm.customer.interests"> Sports
        </label>
        <label class="checkbox-inline">
          <input type="checkbox" value="news"
          data-bind="checked:
          RegistrationForm.customer.interests"> News
        </label>
        <label class="checkbox-inline">
          <input type="checkbox" value="movies"
          data-bind="checked:
          RegistrationForm.customer.interests"> Movies
        </label>
        <label class="checkbox-inline">
```

```
        <input type="checkbox" value="comedy"
        data-bind="checked:
        RegistrationForm.customer.interests"> Comedy
      </label>
    </div>
  </div>
  </div>
</fieldset>
```

We have implemented the fifth feature of our customer registration form application. Open the application in the browser; you should now see the interests section with the checkboxes. Try selecting some interests and click on **Submit**. The selected interests should appear in the console log. The application should look similar to this:

We have reached our fifth checkpoint. The code for this checkpoint can be found at `chapter3\checkpoint5`.

Clearing the registration form

The final feature of our application is to clear the customer registration form. We will add a button, which the customers can click on to clear any input in the form fields. We will add a corresponding method in the module that will clear all observables in the model.

Let's start by updating the view. Next to the Submit button, add a button to view. Label the button Clear. Bind the click event of the button to a method in the module. We will call this method "clear". Your code for button should look similar to this:

```
<button type="button" class="btn btn-default"
data-bind="click: RegistrationForm.clear">Clear</button>
```

Now that we have updated the view, we can add the clear method to our module. Open the model and add the method skeleton. Also, add the method to the return statement of the module. There are a few different ways of clearing the module. You can set the value of each observable in the module by manually calling its setter method. We will use a more generic method, which will traverse the module and check whether the object is an observable. If the object happens to be an observable, we will set its value to null or remove its items if it is an observable array.

 Knockout provides a method, ko.isObservable(obj), which is used to check whether an object is observable or not. It returns true for observables and observable arrays.

We will use a jQuery method called each to traverse the model. This method takes the JSON model to traverse and a function to apply to each node. Inside this function, we can check whether the node is observable and clear its value. The following is the method which uses the jQuery each and Knockout ko.isObservable methods to traverse and clear the model; notice how it handles observable arrays as we cannot set the value of observable arrays to null:

```
/* method to traverse the model and clear observables */
var traverseAndClearModel = function(jsonObj) {
  $.each(jsonObj, function(key,val){
    if(ko.isObservable(val)) {
      if(val.removeAll != undefined) {
        val.removeAll();
      } else {
        val(null);
      }
    } else {
      traverseAndClearModel(val);
    }
  });
};
```

The method checks for the `removeAll` method of observable arrays to distinguish between observables and observable arrays. The method recursively calls itself to visit all the nodes in the model. We will call this method from our `clear` method. The `clear` method will clear the model and add one credit card item to the credit cards array. This method should look similar to this:

```
/* clear the model */
var clear = function () {
  console.log("Clear customer model");
  traverseAndClearModel(customer);
  //add the first credit card
  addCreditCard();
};
```

We have implemented the final feature of our customer registration form application. Open the application in the browser; you should now see the **Clear** button next to the **Submit** button. Try entering information in the form and then click on the **Clear** button to clear the form. We have reached our final checkpoint for this chapter. The code for this checkpoint can be found at `chapter3\checkpoint6`.

Summary

In this chapter, we walked through building a customer registration form. The information captured by the form included personal information, contact details, residential and postal addresses, and credit card information. The application demonstrated Knockout's ability to create a dynamic form. In this chapter, we learned how to use Knockout binding with different form elements.

In the next chapter, we will continue with our customer registration application and apply validation to the different form elements.

4
Adding Validation to the Customer Registration Form

We developed a customer registration form in the previous chapter. While the registration form application demonstrated how to work with form fields, it is missing out on a basic requirement that is expected from most web forms — validation!

In this chapter, we will add validation to our customer registration form application. We will explore two different methods of validating the form data in our model: by using the Knockout extenders and Knockout validation plugin. The chapter will walk you through applying validation to the registration form using the Knockout validation plugin.

It is important to note that the validation we are talking about in this chapter happens at the client side or more specifically, in the browser. The data should also be validated at the server side, but there are some benefits of validating the data at the client side. The benefits are mostly to do with user experience and performance. By validating the data at the client side, we give the users an instant response if they enter invalid inputs. This saves the user from waiting for the HTTP response. It also saves the server from handling requests with invalid data.

Another important concept to note is that the validation is applied to the data in the model and not the HTML form fields that constitute the view.

In this chapter, you will learn how to:

- Validate the model using Knockout extenders
- Validate the model using Knockout validation plugin
- Validate fields based on requirements, such as required minimum and maximum lengths, input types, and input patterns

- Display error styles and messages
- Apply conditional validation
- Apply validation to the dynamically created fields

Validating the model using Knockout extenders

Knockout provides a way to add additional reusable functionality to the observables through the use of extenders. Knockout extenders could be used to add additional properties to the observable or to intercept and rewrite its value. Extenders could also be used to validate the model. This section will explore and demonstrate the use of extenders for validating the model. The example in this section will apply this method of validation only to the first name field.

An extender is created by adding a method to the ko.extenders object. The method takes two parameters: the observable and an option value. The option value is specified when the observable is extended. The method should return an observable. This can either be the observable itself or a computed observable that manipulates the value of the original observable.

Let's create an extender that will extend the firstName observable in our registration form application and mark it as required. The view will display an error style and message if the first name is not set. Apply the following changes to the customer registration form application developed in the previous chapter.

The first step is to add the method to the ko.extenders object. We will call this method required. Our required method looks similar to this:

```
/* extender for required fields */
ko.extenders.required = function(target, option) {
  //observables to indicate an error
  target.hasError = ko.observable(false);

  //set the error flag whenever the value changes
  target.subscribe(function (newValue) {
     target.hasError(newValue ? false : true);
  });

  //return the original observable
  return target;
};
```

Knockout provides a way to add manual subscription to observables through the use of `subscribe` method. This method takes a method as parameter, which is called with the changed value of the observable, every time the value of the observable changes.

The method takes the original observable and option as parameters. The method declares an `hasError` observable as child observable of the original observable. The `hasError` observable is a flag that indicates the error state of the observable. The method adds a subscription to the original observable, which sets the error state based on the value of the observable. An important thing to note is that the subscription will only fire when the value of the observable changes.

 By default, the new value will only be set in the observable when the input field loses focus. This behavior can be changed by using the `valueUpdate` parameter. Options include updating the value of the observable on key press and after key down.

Add the code for `ko.extenders.required` above the declaration for the `customer` model. Now, we can update the `firstName` observable to mark it as required. This is done by the use of the `extend` method on the observable and specifying the name of the extender. You also pass any parameters to the extender. After applying the required extender, the declaration of the `firstName` observable looks similar to this:

```
firstName: ko.observable().extend({ required: null})
```

The next step is to update the view to display the error style and a message if the `firstName` observable is not set. We will use the Bootstrap `has-error` class with the Knockout visible and `css` binding to achieve this. Add the `css` binding to the `div` element surrounding the first name input field. Specify the `has-error` class to the `css` binding if the `hasError` flag is set on the `firstName` observable. Add a `p` element below the first name input field with an appropriate error message. Using the `visible` binding, make it only appear if the `hasError` flag is set on the `firstName` observable. The `div` element containing the first name field should look similar to this:

```
<div class="form-group" data-bind="css: {'has-error':
RegistrationForm.customer.personalInfo.firstName.hasError}">
  <label for="firstNameInput">First Name</label>
  <input type="text" class="form-control" data-bind="value:
  RegistrationForm.customer.personalInfo.firstName"
  id="firstNameInput" placeholder="Enter first name">
  <p class="help-block" data-bind="visible:
  RegistrationForm.customer.personalInfo.firstName.hasError">
  Please enter first name</p>
</div>
```

We have implemented the required field validation on first name. Open the application in the browser. Enter a value in the first name input field. Take the focus away from the field to let the value entered to take effect. Now delete the input in the first name field and move the focus away. You should see the error style and message appear. This is how it appears in our browser:

Registration Form

Personal Information

Title

select ▾

First Name

Enter first name

Please enter first name

Middle Name

Enter middle name

Last Name

Enter last name

The code for this section can be found at `chapter4\ValidationUsingExtenders`.

Validating model using the Knockout validation plugin

Knockout validation is a plugin for validating the model. It uses the Knockout extenders to provide validation, similar to the concept described in the previous section. The advantage of using this plugin is that the most common extenders are already defined for you. All you have to do is configure and apply the extenders. This section will explore and demonstrate the use of the validation plugin for validating the model. The examples in this section will apply this method of validation to all the fields in the customer registration form application. You can make a copy of the customer registration form application developed in the previous chapter and apply the validation by performing the steps in the following sections.

Getting started

The first step is to download the validation plugin. The validation plugin can be downloaded from `https://github.com/Knockout-Contrib/Knockout-Validation`. Place the downloaded files, `knockout.validation.min.js` and `knockout.validation.min.js.map`, in the `javascript` folder. The `javascript` folder should look similar to this:

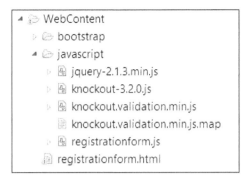

 We have used the minified versions of most JavaScript libraries. Minified JavaScript files increase performance by decreasing time to load. The downside of using minified files is that the code contained in these files is not readable. Most libraries come with normal and minified versions of JavaScript files. Use the normal version if you want to explore the inner workings of the libraries.

We have also used a source map file for the validation plugin. The source map file maps code in the minified JavaScript file to the original unminified version. This helps with debugging the code if an error occurs.

The second step is to include the validation plugin file in your HTML file. Open `registrationform.html` and include the downloaded validation plugin JavaScript file in the `head` element. The head should now look similar to this:

```html
<head>
  <meta http-equiv="Content-Type" content="text/html" />
  <title>Knockout : Registration Form Example</title>

  <link rel="stylesheet" href="bootstrap/css/bootstrap.min.css">

  <script type="text/javascript"
  src="javascript/jquery-2.1.3.min.js"></script>
  <script type="text/javascript"
  src="javascript/knockout-3.2.0.js"></script>
  <script type="text/javascript"
  src="javascript/knockout.validation.min.js"></script>
  <script type="text/javascript"
  src="bootstrap/js/bootstrap.min.js"></script>
  <script type="text/javascript"
  src="javascript/registrationform.js"></script>
</head>
```

We are now ready to use the validation plugin in our application.

The basics

We need to enable the validation plugin in order to start using it. We call the `init` method of the plugin to enable it:

```
// enable validation
ko.validation.init();
```

You can pass parameters to the `init` method to configure the plugin. We will explore this more in the coming section. We will use extenders to apply validation to our observables, similar to the concept described in the previous chapter. To mark an observable as required, simply extend it with the required extender:

```
//myObservable marked as required
var myObservable = ko.observable().extend({ required: true });
```

The following are some other useful extenders; the function of the extenders is pretty self-explanatory from the name:

```
//extender for minimum value
var myObservable = ko.observable().extend({ min: 1 });

//extender for maximum value
var myObservable = ko.observable().extend({ max: 10 });

//extender for minimum length
var myObservable = ko.observable().extend({ minLength: 4 });

//extender for maximum length
var myObservable = ko.observable().extend({ maxLength: 8 });

//extender for number
var myObservable = ko.observable().extend({ number: true });

//extender for email
var myObservable = ko.observable().extend({ email: true });

//extender for date
var myObservable = ko.observable().extend({ date: true });

//extender for pattern matching.
var myObservable = ko.observable().extend({ pattern: '^[0-9]*$'
});
```

You can apply multiple extenders like this:

```
//required with a minimum length of 5
var myObservable = ko.observable().extend({ required: true,
minLength: 5});
```

You can also chain multiple extenders together. The following example chains the required and minimum length together:

```
//required with a minimum length of 5 by chaining
var myObservable = ko.observable().extend({ required:
true}).extend({minLength: 5});
```

The plugin comes with default error messages. You can specify a custom error message by using the message property of the extenders, for example:

```
//custom error message for required field
var myObservable = ko.observable().extend({ required: { params:
true, message: "Please enter a value for this field."}});
```

You can use the `group` method provided by the plugin to capture the validation results in the object returned. This will give us the ability to check whether our model is valid or not in the `submit` method. The returned object also gives us some useful methods, for example, a method called `showAllMessages` to highlight all the errors. The `group` method takes the model optional configuration object as parameters. In the following example, we indicate to the `group` method that our model has observables that are nested by setting the `deep` attribute to `true`. This will cause the `group` method to traverse each node of our model in search of observables with extenders:

```
//group error by deep scanning
myModel.errors = ko.validation.group(myModel, { deep: true });
```

Now that we have learned the basics of the validation plugin, let's apply validation to our customer registration form.

Validating personal information

The requirement for validating personal information is that the title, first name, and last name fields are mandatory. Middle name is optional, so we will not apply any validation to it. We will use the Bootstrap error styles and Knockout validation plugins default messages to highlight the errors. You should have downloaded and included the Knockout validation plugin if you followed the *Getting started* section of this chapter. Remember that we are picking up the customer registration form application from where we left it at the end of the previous chapter.

The first step is to initialize and configure the validation plugin. We will add the initialization and configuration in a method. This method will be called from our init method of the module. Open the `registrationform.js` file and add the following method to the module:

```
/* method to configure the validation plugin */
var configureValidation = function () {
  //initialize and configure the validation plugin
  ko.validation.init({
    errorElementClass: 'has-error',
    errorMessageClass: 'help-block'
  });
  //group errors
  customer.errors = ko.validation.group(customer, {deep:true});
};
```

The preceding method initializes the validation plugin so that we can start using the plugin and also configures it to use the Bootstrap error classes for styling the fields.

 To style elements to indicate an error, Bootstrap provides the 'has-error' and 'help-block' CSS classes.

The method, in its second line, groups the errors to customer.errors. Notice that we specify that our model has nested observables by passing in the deep attribute as true. We can now call the configureValidation method from the init method of the module. Your init method should now look similar to this:

```
var init = function () {
  /* add code to initialize this module */
  //configure validation
  configureValidation();
  //add the first credit card
  addCreditCard();
  //apply ko bindings
  ko.applyBindings(RegistrationForm);
};
```

The next step is to modify our submit method to check whether our model is valid or not. This can be achieved by checking for the number of errors. We want to highlight all the error fields if errors exist, otherwise, we proceed as normal. Here is the updated submit method to achieve this:

```
/* form submission */
var submit = function () {
```

```
   if (customer.errors().length === 0) {
     console.log("Customer model is valid.");
     console.log(ko.toJSON(customer));
   } else {
     console.log("Customer model has errors.");
     //highlight all errors
     customer.errors.showAllMessages();
   }
};
```

Now we can apply the required validation to the first and last name fields. We will tackle the title fields after that as it is slightly more complicated. Add the required extender to the first and last name observables in our model. The following is an example of how to apply the required extender to the `firstName` observable:

```
firstName: ko.observable().extend({ required: true})
```

We are now ready to modify the view. Open the `registrationform.html` file and locate the first and last name input fields. All we need to do is specify the `validationElement` data binding to the surrounding `div` element. The Following is an example of first name field; the last name field must be modified in the same manner:

```
<div class="form-group" data-bind="validationElement:
RegistrationForm.customer.personalInfo.firstName">
  <label for="firstNameInput">First Name</label>
  <input type="text" class="form-control" data-bind="value:
  RegistrationForm.customer.personalInfo.firstName"
  id="firstNameInput" placeholder="Enter first name">
</div>
```

Open the application in the browser. Try submitting a form without entering anything in the first and last name input fields. You should see the error message and styles appear. You should also see the error message appear in the console logs.

Let's apply the validation to the `title` field. This is slightly more complicated as the `title` input field is a Bootstrap dropdown and consists of multiple components. Start by adding the required extender to the `title` observable in the model, similar to the first and last name. It should look similar to this:

```
title: ko.observable().extend({ required: true})
```

Now, we will update the view to apply the error styles to the title dropdown. First, we bind the surrounding div element with the validationElement data binding, similar to the first and last name surrounding div elements. We then have to add the form-control class to the button. This will tell Bootstrap that it has to apply the error styles to this element. We also modify the row columns and the alignment of the button text. We then make the most important change, which is to add the error message. We did not have to do this for the first and last name as Knockout validation plugin automatically adds it after the input element. We have to manually add this since the title field does not use an input element. To add the error message, we use a span element with the validationMessage data binding. After making the modifications, the title div should look similar to this:

```
<div class="form-group" data-bind="validationElement:
RegistrationForm.customer.personalInfo.title">
  <label for="titleInput">Title</label>
  <div class="dropdown">
    <button class="btn btn-default dropdown-toggle form-control"
    type="button" id="titleInput" data-toggle="dropdown"
    aria-expanded="true">
      <div class="pull-left">
        <span data-bind="text: RegistrationForm.titleSelect">
        </span>
        <span class="caret"></span>
      </div>
    </button>
    <ul class="dropdown-menu" role="menu"
    aria-labelledby="titleInput" data-bind="foreach:
    RegistrationForm.titleOptions">
      <li role="presentation"><a role="menuitem" tabindex="-1"
      data-bind="text: value, click: setTitle"></a></li>
    </ul>
  </div>
  <span class="help-block" data-bind="validationMessage:
  RegistrationForm.customer.personalInfo.title"></span>
</div>
```

Open the application in the browser and try hitting **Submit** without entering any information in the form fields. You should see the error messages and error styles appear for the title, first name, and last name fields. Try entering the missing information and see what happens. In my browser, it looks similar to the following screenshot:

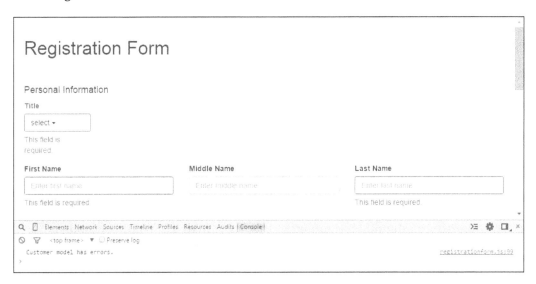

We have reached our first checkpoint for validating the model using Knockout validation plugin. The code for this checkpoint can be found at `chapter4\ValidationUsingPlugin\checkpoint1`.

Validating contact details

The contact details for our customer registration form consists of a phone number, an e-mail address, and a preferred contact. The requirements are to make these three fields as required information. In addition to this, the phone number should only consist of numbers, with minimum length of four and maximum length of nine. The e-mail should be syntactically valid.

Let's start with modifying the module by adding the extenders to the contact details observables. Open the module and add an extender to the `phoneNumber` observable and mark it as required, with a minimum length of four, maximum length of nine, and a number type. Add an extender to the `email` observable and mark it as required and of type, e-mail. Similarly, add an extender to the `preferredContact` observable and mark it as required. The contact details part of your model should look similar to this:

```
contactDetails: {
  phoneNumber: ko.observable().extend({ required: true, minLength:
  4, maxLength: 9, number: true}),
  emailAddress: ko.observable().extend({ required: true, email:
  true}),
  preferredContact: ko.observable().extend({ required: true})
}
```

Now we can modify our view to add the validation to these fields. Modifications to the phone number and e-mail is pretty straightforward. All you need to do is add the `validationElement` data binding to the surrounding `div` elements of these fields. Go ahead and add the data binding to the phone number and e-mail fields. The phone number `div` should look similar to this; the e-mail `div` would be similar:

```
<div class="form-group" data-bind="validationElement:
RegistrationForm.customer.contactDetails.phoneNumber">
  <label for="phoneNumberInput">Phone Number</label>
  <input type="text" class="form-control" data-bind="value:
  RegistrationForm.customer.contactDetails.phoneNumber"
  id="phoneNumberInput" placeholder="Enter phone number">
</div>
```

The preferred contact is slightly more complicated. If you apply the `validationElement` data binding to the surrounding `div` of the preferred contact, you end up with the error messages for both the radio button, as shown in the following screenshot (this is because the validation plugin will automatically insert error messages after every `input` element):

The behavior we want to achieve is that the error message only appears once at the bottom of the radio buttons. To do this, we need to tell the validation plugin not to insert the messages for this field by using the `validationOptions` data binding with `insertMessages` set to `false`. We then specify the location of the message by using the `validationMessage` data binding. Go ahead and apply the changes described in the preceding section. You should end up with the preferred contact section of the view looking similar to this:

```
<div class="col-md-6">
  <label>Preferred Contact</label>
  <div class="form-group" data-bind="validationElement:
  RegistrationForm.customer.contactDetails.preferredContact,
  validationOptions: {insertMessages: false}">
    <label class="radio-inline">
      <input type="radio" value="phone"
      name="preferredContactInput" data-bind="checked:
      RegistrationForm.customer.contactDetails.preferredContact">
      Phone
    </label>
    <label class="radio-inline">
      <input type="radio" value="email"
      name="preferredContactInput" data-bind="checked:
      RegistrationForm.customer.contactDetails.preferredContact">
      Email
    </label>
    <span class="help-block" data-bind="validationMessage:
    RegistrationForm.customer.contactDetails.preferredContact">
    </span>
  </div>
</div>
```

Open the application in the browser and try hitting **Submit** without entering any information in the form fields. You should see the error messages and error styles appear for the phone number, e-mail, and preferred contact fields. Try entering invalid e-mail address and non-number characters for phone number. In my browser, it should look similar to this:

We have reached our second checkpoint for validating the model using the Knockout validation plugin. The code for this checkpoint can be found at `chapter4\ValidationUsingPlugin\checkpoint1`.

Validating address details

The address details section of the customer registration form has two parts: residential address and postal address. Postal address can be either street address or PO Box address. The requirements for validating residential address is pretty straightforward. All the fields for residential address are required. The post code is a number with a maximum length of four. Similar requirements apply to the postal street and PO Box addresses, the difference being that the validation for postal address fields is conditional, based on the type of postal address. If the postal address is of the type street, the street address fields should be validated. If the postal address is of the type PO Box, the PO Box address fields should be validated.

Let's start with validating the residential address fields. This is similar to what we have done for the personal information and contact details fields. Modify the observables in the model for residential address to add the validation extenders. Make all the fields required. Mark the `postCode` as a number and give it a maximum length of four. The residential address in the model should look similar to this:

```
residential: {
  street: ko.observable().extend({ required: true}),
  city: ko.observable().extend({ required: true}),
  postCode: ko.observable().extend({ required: true, maxLength: 4,
  number: true}),
  country: ko.observable().extend({ required: true})
},
```

Now modify the corresponding fields in the view and add the `validationElement` data bindings to the surrounding `div` elements of the fields. The following is an example of the street field; the other fields for residential address should be similar:

```
<div class="form-group" data-bind="validationElement:
RegistrationForm.customer.address.residential.street">
  <label for="streetInput">Street Address</label>
  <input type="text" class="form-control" data-bind="value:
  RegistrationForm.customer.address.residential.street"
  id="streetInput" placeholder="Enter street address">
</div>
```

Open the application in the browser and make sure that the validation for the residential address works as expected after making the changes described. In our browser, it looks similar to this:

Now let's move on to validating the postal address and a slightly more complicated scenario of conditional validation. We want to validate the street address fields if the postal address is of the type street. Similarly, we want to validate the PO Box fields if the postal address is of the type PO Box. Let's start by applying validation to both the street address and PO Box address fields and see what behavior we get in the application. This will make us appreciate why conditional validation is important.

Apply validation to both the street address and PO Box address fields by adding the extenders to the observables in our module and modifying the corresponding fields in the view and adding the `validationElement` data bindings. You should be able to do this by following the example of validating the residential address. Open the application in the browser after you have applied the validation to the street address and PO Box address fields. Select postal address type by clicking either the **Street Address** or the **PO Box** radio button. Try submitting the form without entering any information for the postal address. You should see that the form has errors. Try populating the postal address fields and submit the form. You should still see errors in the console log. This is because the errors are on the fields of postal address, which are not in current view. Switch the postal address type to see the fields with the errors. We will use conditional validation to solve this problem. This is done by specifying when the validation should take place by using the `onlyIf` parameter of the `required` extender. The `onlyIf` parameter takes a method, which should return a `true` if the validation is required and `false` if the validation is not. The following example shows the street observable with conditional validation if address type is street:

```
var streetObservable = ko.observable().extend({ required: { onlyIf
: function () {
  return addressType == "street";
}}});
```

Let's apply conditional validation to our postal address types by using the `onlyIf` parameter. As our conditional validation depends on the `type` attribute in our model, we have to apply the conditional validation after the model is declared, and not during declaration as we did in the previous example. We will write a method that will apply the conditional validation. This method can then be called when the validation plugin is being configured. First, we write helper methods that return either a `true` or a `false`, depending on the type of postal address. Here is a simple implementation of these methods:

```
/* returns true if postal address is of type street */
var isStreetAddress = function () {
  return customer.address.postal.type() == "street";
};


/* returns true if postal address is of type pobox */
var isPoBoxAddress = function () {
  return customer.address.postal.type() == "pobox";
};
```

Now we will write a method to apply the conditional validation to the postal address fields using the `onlyIf` property and the helper methods we described in the preceding section. The method should look similar to this:

```
/* method applies conditional validation to the model */
var applyConditionalValidation = function () {
  //postal street address fields
  customer.address.postal.streetAddress.street.extend({ required:
  {onlyIf: isStreetAddress}});
  customer.address.postal.streetAddress.city.extend({ required:
  {onlyIf: isStreetAddress}});
  customer.address.postal.streetAddress.postCode.extend({
  required: {onlyIf: isStreetAddress}});
  customer.address.postal.streetAddress.country.extend({ required:
  {onlyIf: isStreetAddress}});

  //postal PO Box address fields
  customer.address.postal.poBoxAddress.poBox.extend({ required:
  {onlyIf: isPoBoxAddress}});
  customer.address.postal.poBoxAddress.city.extend({ required:
  {onlyIf: isPoBoxAddress}});
  customer.address.postal.poBoxAddress.postCode.extend({ required:
  {onlyIf: isPoBoxAddress}});
  customer.address.postal.poBoxAddress.country.extend({ required:
  {onlyIf: isPoBoxAddress}});
};
```

The method applies the required extender with the `onlyIf` parameter to the postal address fields. An important point to note is that we do not apply the `required` extender during our model declaration when applying conditional validation that depends on another field in the same model. The model should look similar to this:

```
postal: {
  type: ko.observable(),
  streetAddress: {
    street: ko.observable(),
    city: ko.observable(),
    postCode: ko.observable().extend({ maxLength: 4, number:
    true}),
    country: ko.observable()
  },
  poBoxAddress: {
    poBox:  ko.observable().extend({ maxLength: 6, number: true}),
    city: ko.observable(),
    postCode: ko.observable().extend({ maxLength: 4, number:
    true}),
    country: ko.observable()
  }
}
```

Now, we can call the `applyConditionalValidation` method from our `configureValidation` method below the validation plugin initialization.

One last step is to validate the postal address `type` field. This is similar to the preferred contact field validation. Modify the `type` field of the postal address to mark it as required and then modify the corresponding section in the view by applying the `validationElement`, `validationOptions`, and the `validationMessage` data binding.

Try running the application after applying the preceding steps described. Try different combinations of street and PO Box addresses, and see how it affects the validation. You should see the conditional validation on the street and PO Box postal address. With PO Box selected as the postal address type, it looks similar to this in our browser:

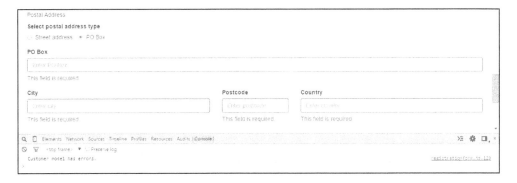

We have reached our third checkpoint for validating the model using the Knockout validation plugin. The code for this checkpoint can be found at `chapter4\ValidationUsingPlugin\checkpoint1`.

Validating credit cards

The requirement for validating credit card is that all the three fields—name, number, and expiry date—are required. In addition to that, the credit card number should be of the type number and the expiry date should be of the format "mm/yy". This would have been simple to implement if we were dealing with statically defined fields as was the case with our previous examples. In the case of credit cards, we have to tackle the fields that are dynamically defined.

We will use most of the same concepts of the extenders, validation groups, and validation data bindings as before. The only difference is that the extenders and validation groups will have to be dynamically created. Let's start by modifying the credit card model in the module to dynamically add the extenders. We will also create a validation group for the new credit card object. Locate the `addCreditCard` method in the module. Refactor the method to pull the credit card object, pushed to the `creditCards` observable array. Now add the appropriate extenders to the observables. Create a validation group by using the `ko.validation.group` method and store the group returned on the credit card object. The refactored `addCreditCard` method should look similar to this:

```
/* method to add credit card to the credit cards array */
var addCreditCard = function () {
  //create the card object
  var card = { name: ko.observable().extend({ required: true}),
          number: ko.observable().extend({ required: true, number:
          true}),
          expiryDate: ko.observable().extend({ required: true,
          pattern: '^(0[1-9]|1[012])/\\d\\d$'})};
  //create the validation group for the card
  card.errors = ko.validation.group(card);
  //add the newly created card to the array
  customer.creditCards.push(card);
};
```

The preceding code creates the card object with the `required` extender for all the fields. It uses the `number` extender to mark the number field as a number type. It also uses the `pattern` extender to validate the date format.

Now, we can update the view to add the `validationElement` data binding to the corresponding fields. Locate the section in the view that renders the credit cards. Add the `validationElement` data binding to the credit card fields. Here is an example of the name field; the number and expiry date fields should look similar:

```
<div class="form-group" data-bind="validationElement: name">
  <label for="ccNameInput">Name on card</label>
  <input type="text" class="form-control" data-bind="value: name"
  id="ccNameInput" placeholder="Enter name on card">
</div>
```

The last step is to refactor the `submit` method in the module to display any errors that exist for credit cards. To do this, you will have to loop through the credit card array and check the individual card. Call the `showAllMessages` method on the error group of the card object if errors exist. Let's make these changes by creating a new method. The method will return `false` if any of the credit card fields have an error. It will also show the errors on the view. If you have a go at writing the method, you can use the `ko.utils.arrayForEach` method to loop through the credit card array. Your method should look similar to this:

```
/* method returns false if any of the credit cards have
 * errors, true otherwise
 * method also calls show all message on the card object
 */
var checkCeditCardsForErrors = function () {
  var valid = true;
  ko.utils.arrayForEach(customer.creditCards(), function(card) {
    if(card.errors().length > 0) {
      valid = false;
      card.errors.showAllMessages();
    }
  });
  return valid;
};
```

We will also pull the logic to check for errors in the static fields out of the `submit` method to make the code more simple and maintainable. This new method also returns either a true or a false based on the error state of the static fields. It looks similar to this:

```
/* method return false if any of the static fields
 * have errors, true otherwise
 * method also calls show all messages on the static fields
 */
var checkStaticFIeldsForErrors = function () {
```

```
    if (customer.errors().length > 0) {
      customer.errors.showAllMessages();
      return false;
    }
    return true;
  };
```

Finally, modify the `submit` method to use the two new methods we created to check for errors in the credit card and static fields. The modified submit method should look similar to this:

```
/* form submission */
var submit = function () {
  var creditCardError = checkCeditCardsForErrors();
  var staticFieldError = checkStaticFIeldsForErrors();

  if(creditCardError && staticFieldError) {
    console.log("Customer model is valid.");
    console.log(ko.toJSON(customer));
  } else {
    console.log("Customer model has errors.");
  }
};
```

Try running the application after applying the preceding steps. Submit the form without entering any information for credit cards. Now add additional cards and see what happens. In our browser, it looks similar to this:

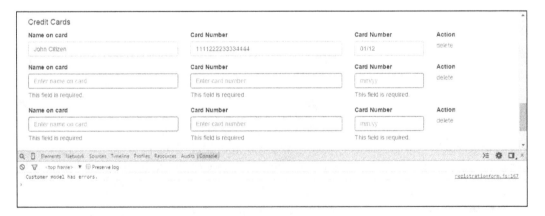

We have reached the final checkpoint for validating the model using the Knockout validation plugin. The code for this checkpoint can be found at `chapter4\ValidationUsingPlugin\checkpoint1`.

Summary

In this chapter, we walked through adding validation to the customer registration form we built in the previous chapter. The chapter looked at two different techniques of applying validation. We first explored validating the model using custom extenders. We defined the required extender and learned how to apply error styles using the `visible` and `css` bindings. We applied validation to the first name field using our custom extender.

The second part of the chapter looked at applying validation to the model using the Knockout validation plugin. This part of the chapter walked you through the customer registration form and applied validation to the personal information, contact details, address, and credit card fields. We learned how to apply validation to static and dynamically created fields. We also learned how to apply conditional validation.

The next chapter is a first in a series of three on building a customer banking portal. In this chapter, we will learn how to build some of the user interface components required in a complex real-world application.

5
Creating a Customer Banking Portal

Let us assume a fictional bank, referred to as MyBank, for the purpose of developing the customer banking portal in this and the next two chapter. The governance board of MyBank has decided that its time the bank goes digital. The board wants the bank to maintain market relevance by offering online services to its members. It wants to provide its members with an easy to use, responsive, rich, and secure online portal. The CIO of MyBank has contacted you to develop the online portal. The CIO wants to take an iterative approach to developing this application, and has given you the following user stories to implement for the first release:

- As a member, I want to easily navigate between different features of the portal
- As a member, I want to view the contact details and information about the bank
- As a member, I want to view my accounts
- As a member, I want to view the transactions I have made for an account
- As a member, I want to view my personal information

This chapter will walk you through designing and developing the customer banking portal application for MyBank. The customer banking portal application will build upon the concepts we have learned so far in the previous chapters such as working with observables, observable arrays, and forms. In addition, we will learn how to use some of the navigation constructs such as navigation bars and tab containers.

In this chapter, we will learn how to:

- Build navigation into your application using a navigation bar
- Use a tab container to structure content and application features
- Construct master details view using tables

As mandated by the CIO of MyBank, we will be taking an iterative approach to building the application. Each user story or feature will have a corresponding checkpoint folder in the accompanying code. The folders are named `chapter5\checkpoint1`, `chapter5\checkpoint2`, and so on.

 Mike Cohn describes **user story** as a short and simple description of a feature told from the perspective of the person who desires the new capability, usually a user or customer of the system. You can find out more about user stories and other agile topics on his website at `http://www.mountaingoatsoftware.com/agile`.

Creating the skeleton

We will create the skeleton for the application before we can start developing the first feature of the customer banking portal. You should be familiar with how to create a skeleton from the previous chapters.

Create the folder structure and copy the relevant Knockout and Bootstrap files. Create `bankportal.html` file under the `WebContent` folder. This file will hold our view. The contents of this file should look similar to this:

```
<!DOCTYPE HTML>
<html>
  <head>
    <meta http-equiv="Content-Type" content="text/html" />
    <title>Knockout : Customer banking portal</title>

    <link rel="stylesheet" href="bootstrap/css/bootstrap.min.css">

    <script type="text/javascript"
    src="javascript/jquery-2.1.3.min.js"></script>
    <script type="text/javascript"
    src="javascript/knockout-3.2.0.js"></script>
    <script type="text/javascript"
    src="javascript/knockout.validation.min.js"></script>
    <script type="text/javascript"
    src="bootstrap/js/bootstrap.min.js"></script>
```

```
    <script type="text/javascript"
    src="javascript/bankportal.js"></script>
  </head>
  <body>
    <div class="container">
      <!-- content -->
    </div>
  </body>
</html>
```

Now create the JavaScript file to hold our application module. We will call it `bankportal.js`. Add a skeleton module to the file. The skeleton module should look similar to this:

```
/* Module for Customer banking portal application */
var BankPortal = function () {

/* add members here */

/* the model */
  var member = {
};

  /* method to initialize the module */
  var init = function () {
    /* add code to initialize this module */
    //apply ko bindings
    ko.applyBindings(BankPortal);
  };

  /* execute the init function when the DOM is ready */
  $(init);

  return {
    /* add members that will be exposed publicly */
    member: member
  };
}();
```

The resulting folder structure should look similar to this:

View the application in the browser. It should give you a page with the page header. We are now ready to start developing the user stories.

Let's get started and build the first user story of the customer banking portal.

Navigating between application features

The first user story states that the application should make it easier for the members to navigate between different application features of the portal. We get an idea of the application features from the rest of the user stories. The main application features are the ability to view information about the bank, the contact details, account and transactions, and personal information. We will divide the screen based on these features using a navigation bar and a tab container. The navigation bar will be used to navigate between information about the bank, contact details, and a home page. The home page will further divide features such as the ability to view accounts and details and personal information.

The description of the navigation is depicted in the following wireframe:

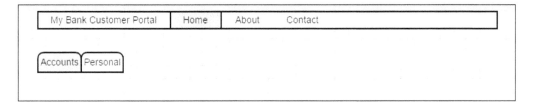

 A **wireframe** is a page schematic or a visual design that depicts the user interface components and the page layout. Wireframes help in communicating the visual design and site functionality to the developers.

Let's get started by developing the navigation bar. We will use the HTML nav element for the top navigation bar. The styling for the navigation bar is provided by Bootstrap. Open the view in the bankportal.html file and use the nav element to create the navigation bar. The navigation bar should have a header and the three navigation options specified in the wireframe. The nav element should be the first element in the div container. With the Bootstrap styling applied, our nav element looks similar to this:

```
<nav class="navbar navbar-default">
  <div class="container-fluid">
    <div class="navbar-header">
      <p class="navbar-text">My Bank Customer Portal</p>
    </div>
    <div id="navbar" class="navbar-collapse collapse">
      <ul class="nav navbar-nav">
        <li class="active">
          <a href="#">Home</a>
        </li>
        <li>
          <a href="#">About</a>
        </li>
        <li>
          <a href="#">Contact</a>
        </li>
      </ul>
    </div>
  </div>
</nav>
```

View the application in the browser. You should see a page with a navigation bar at the top with the three navigation options. Try clicking on the navigation options and see what happens. If you want the navigation bar to be responsive, resize and adjust it to the screen size. Next, add the following code to the `div` element with the `navbar-header` class before the `p` element containing the header text:

```
<button type="button" class="navbar-toggle collapsed"
data-toggle="collapse" data-target="#navbar" aria-expanded="false"
aria-controls="navbar">
<span class="sr-only">Toggle navigation</span>
  <span class="icon-bar"></span>
  <span class="icon-bar"></span>
  <span class="icon-bar"></span>
</button>
```

View the application in the browser again. Try reducing the size of the browser window or view the application from a mobile device. You should see the navigation options disappear and a button appear. Click the button to see the navigation options.

So far, we have implemented the navigation bar, but it really doesn't do much. Let's give it dynamic behavior by adding a `click` binding to each navigation option, which will show or hide the related view. The views for home, about, and contact can be the `div` elements for now with place holder text. To add this dynamic behavior, we first create an observable in our module that will hold the active page. The active page is the page selected by the user by clicking on the navigation option. We then add a method to the module to set the active page when the navigation is clicked upon by using the `click` binding. To achieve this, add the following code in the module:

```
/* attribute to hold the active page */
var activePage = ko.observable("Home");

/* method to set the active page */
var setActivePage = function (page) {
  console.log("Setting active page to: " + page);
  activePage(page);
};
```

Now, add the `click` bindings to the anchor elements for home, about, and contact. Pass the name of the active page to the `setActivePage` method. The `click` binding should look similar to this:

```
<div id="navbar" class="navbar-collapse collapse">
  <ul class="nav navbar-nav">
    <li class="active">
      <a href="#" data-bind="click:
      BankPortal.setActivePage.bind($data, 'Home')">Home</a>
    </li>
    <li>
      <a href="#" data-bind="click:
      BankPortal.setActivePage.bind($data, 'About')">About</a>
    </li>
    <li>
      <a href="#" data-bind="click:
      BankPortal.setActivePage.bind($data, 'Contact')">Contact</a>
    </li>
  </ul>
</div>
```

Notice the way we are passing the name of the page to the `setActivePage` method in the click binding. The `bind` method attaches the parameter value to the function reference. In our case, it will create a new function with a fixed argument, the name of the page, and attach it to our module referenced by `$data`. Try running the application in the browser and click on the navigation options. You should be able to see the active page observable change by viewing the console logs.

The next step is to write a method in our module that we can use to check whether a page is active or not. The method will take the name of the page as parameter and return true if it matches to the active page, otherwise, it will return `true`. The method could look similar to the following code; add `setActivePage` and `isActivePage` methods to the `return` statement of the module so that they are accessible form the view:

```
/* returns true if parameter matches
   active page, false otherwise */
var isActivePage = function (page) {
  return activePage() === page;
}
```

Now, we can add the views for the navigation pages. For now, these can be just `div` elements with place holder text. The active page is made visible by using the `visible` binding. The navigation pages should look similar to this:

```
<div id="home" data-bind="visible: BankPortal.isActivePage('Home')">
   <p>--- Content for Home goes here ---</p>
</div>
<div id="about" data-bind="visible: BankPortal.isActivePage('About')">
   <p>--- Content for About goes here ---</p>
</div>
<div id="contact" data-bind="visible: BankPortal.
isActivePage('Contact')">
   <p>--- Content for Contact goes here ---</p>
</div>
```

Notice that we are not using the `bind` function to pass the name of the page to the `isActivePage` method. The `bind` function is only required to pass arguments to methods when using the `click` binding. Try running the application in the browser and click on the navigation options. You should see the views change based on the navigation option clicked. You might also notice that the navigation option selected is not highlighted to tell the user that it is active. Let's fix this by adding a `css` binding to the active navigation. We will make use of our `isActivePage` method again. The following is an example of the home navigation option. Update the navigation options based on this example:

```
<li data-bind="css: {active: BankPortal.isActivePage('Home')}">
   <a href="#" data-bind="click:
   BankPortal.setActivePage.bind($data, 'Home')">Home</a>
</li>
```

Try running the application after applying the step described earlier. You should be able to navigate using the options in the navigation bar. So far, in our browser, it looks similar to the following screenshot:

The second part of the navigation feature is to develop tabs for accounts and personal information. We will develop two tabs, which are specified by the wireframe—accounts and personal. Developing the tabs container is similar to the navigation bar we created in the earlier section. Similar to page navigation using the navigation bar, we will need an observable in our module that will track the active tab. We also need methods to set the active tab and to check whether the tab is active or not. To achieve this, add the following code to the module; add the `setActiveTab` and `isActiveTab` methods to the return statement of the module:

```
/* attribute to hold the active tab */
var activeTab = ko.observable("Accounts");

/* method to set the active tab */
var setActiveTab = function (tab) {
  console.log("Setting active tab to: " + tab);
  activeTab(tab);
};

/* returns true if parameter matches
   active tab, false otherwise */
var isActiveTab = function (tab) {
  return activeTab() === tab;
}
```

Now that we have the methods in our module to support the tabs container, let's update our view. The tabs container should go in the `div` element for the home page. We use the Bootstrap `nav` and `nav-tabs` classes on HTML list to create the tabs, similar to the navigation bar. Each list item will have an anchor with a `click` binding to set the active tab by using the `setActiveTab` method and passing the name of the tab as a parameter. Remember to use the `bind` function when passing a parameter using the `click` binding. The list item will also have a `css` binding to set the active tab. The `css` binding should use the `isActiveTab` method and pass the name of the tab as a parameter.

Create the views for accounts and personal using `div` elements. These views can have place holder text for now. Use the visible binding on the `div` elements to show hide the contents for the active tab. These views should go below the tabs container. The `div` element for the home page should look similar to this:

```
<div id="home" data-bind="visible: BankPortal.isActivePage('Home')">
  <ul class="nav nav-tabs">
    <li data-bind="css: {active:
    BankPortal.isActiveTab('Accounts')}">
```

```
        <a href="#" data-bind="click:
        BankPortal.setActiveTab.bind($data,
        'Accounts')">Accounts</a>
    </li>
    <li data-bind="css: {active:
    BankPortal.isActiveTab('Personal')}">
        <a href="#" data-bind="click:
        BankPortal.setActiveTab.bind($data,
        'Personal')">Personal</a>
    </li>
</ul>
<div id="accounts" data-bind="visible:
BankPortal.isActiveTab('Accounts')">
    <p>--- Content for Accounts goes here ---</p>
</div>
<div id="personal" data-bind="visible:
BankPortal.isActiveTab('Personal')">
    <p>--- Content for Personal goes here ---</p>
</div>
</div>
```

Open the application in the browser. Try switching through the different navigation options. You should now see the tabs container under the home page. Try switching through the two tab options of accounts and personal. In our browser, it should look similar to this:

We have reached our first checkpoint. The code for this checkpoint can be found at chapter5\checkpoint1.

Viewing contact details and information about the bank

The second user story states that the application should provide the ability to the user to view contact details and information about the bank. We have already developed the about and contact details pages as part of the first story. All we have to do now is to add content to the relevant sections.

The requirements for the contact details, specified by the client, are relatively straightforward. We need to display contact details for general enquires and lost or damaged card. We will use the Bootstrap panel to display this information. Open the view and create a `div` element for the panel to display the contact details for general enquiry. This `div` element goes in the section we created for the contact page earlier that contained the place holder text. Add the panel heading and body by using the `panel-heading` and `panel-body` CSS styles. Add contact details; you can make up the phone numbers and operating hours. Surround the panel with a `div` element and grid CSS to make it responsive. After adding panels for both general enquiries and lost or damaged cards, our code looks similar to this:

```
<div id="contact" data-bind="visible:
BankPortal.isActivePage('Contact')">
  <div class="row">
    <div class="col-md-6">
      <div class="panel panel-default">
        <div class="panel-heading">General enquiries</div>
        <div class="panel-body">
          <p>Call us: 111 1111 </br> 24 hours a day</p>
          <p>Calling from overseas? </br>
          Call us: +000111 111111 </br> 24 hours a day</p>
        </div>
      </div>
    </div>
    <div class="col-md-6">
      <div class="panel panel-default">
        <div class="panel-heading">Lost or damaged card</div>
        <div class="panel-body">
          <p>Call us: 111 2222 </br> 24 hours a day</p>
          <p>Calling from overseas? </br>
          Call us: +000111 222222 </br> 24 hours a day</p>
        </div>
      </div>
    </div>
  </div>
</div>
```

Open the application in the browser and navigate to the contact page. It should look similar to this:

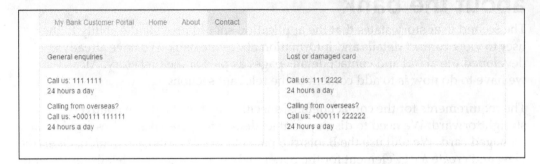

The requirements for displaying information about the bank, as specified by the client, is slightly more complicated. The client wants to display three pieces of information; open an account, lost cards, and make a donation. The clients wants to display this information in a carousel. To satisfy the requirement, we will use the carousel component from Bootstrap. Add the following code to the about section of the view—the div element with the about ID:

```
<div id="myBankCarousel" class="carousel slide"
data-ride="carousel">
  <!-- Indicators -->
  <ol class="carousel-indicators">
    <li data-target="#myBankCarousel" data-slide-to="0"
    class="active"></li>
    <li data-target="#myBankCarousel" data-slide-to="1"
    class=""></li>
    <li data-target="#myBankCarousel" data-slide-to="2"
    class=""></li>
  </ol>
  <div class="carousel-inner" role="listbox">
    <div class="item active">
      <div class="container">
        <div class="carousel-caption">
          <h1>Open an account online in minutes</h1>
          <p>No need to visit a branch! No more waiting in
          queues!</p>
          <p>
            <a class="btn btn-default" href="#" role="button">Sign
            up today</a>
          </p>
        </div>
```

```
      </div>
    </div>
    <div class="item">
      <div class="container">
        <div class="carousel-caption">
          <h1>Lost your card?</h1>
          <p>Report your lost card online and we will send you a
          new one!</p>
          <p>
            <a class="btn btn-default" href="#"
            role="button">Learn more</a>
          </p>
        </div>
      </div>
    </div>
    <div class="item">
      <div class="container">
        <div class="carousel-caption">
          <h1>Make a donation</h1>
          <p>Make a donation online through us to your favourite
          charity.</p>
          <p>
            <a class="btn btn-default" href="#"
            role="button">Donate</a>
          </p>
        </div>
      </div>
    </div>
  </div>
  <a class="left carousel-control" href="#myBankCarousel"
  role="button" data-slide="prev">
    <span class="glyphicon glyphicon-chevron-left"
    aria-hidden="true"></span>
    <span class="sr-only">Previous</span>
  </a>
  <a class="right carousel-control" href="#myBankCarousel"
  role="button" data-slide="next">
    <span class="glyphicon glyphicon-chevron-right"
    aria-hidden="true"></span>
    <span class="sr-only">Next</span>
  </a>
</div>
```

The next step is to create a CSS file called `carousel.css` and include it in the view. This file will hold styles to customize the carousel. If the CSS file is created in the `css` folder, the inclusion should look similar to this:

```
<link rel="stylesheet" href="css/carousel.css">
```

This file should be included after the CSS for Bootstrap as it overrides some styles. Open the newly created `carousel.css` file and add the following content:

```css
/* ------ CUSTOMIZE THE CAROUSEL ------ */
.carousel {
  height: 300px;
  margin-bottom: 60px;
}
.carousel-caption {
  color: #a8a8a8;
}
.carousel .item {
  height: 300px;
  background-color: #f7f7f7;
}
.carousel-indicators li {
  background-color: #a8a8a8;
  border: 1px solid #979797;
}
.carousel-indicators .active {
  border: 1px solid #979797;
}
```

Let's take a minute to go through what we have done. We created a carousel component using Bootstrap. This component is `div` with the `myBankCarousel` ID. The ID is mandatory for this component for the controls to function properly. The `carousel` class on the `div` element specifies that this is a carousel. The `slide` class specifies the CSS transition and animation effects. The list element with the `carousel-indicators` class are responsible for displaying the little dots at the bottom of the carousel to indicate the active item. The slide items are created in the `div` element with the `carousel-inner` class. Each item is a `div` element with the `item` class. The controls to move the carousel left or right are specified by the anchor elements with the `left` or `right` classes and the `carousel-control` class.

Try running the application in your browser and go to the about page. You should see the carousel component. Try navigating by using the left and the right buttons. It looks similar to the following screenshot in our browser:

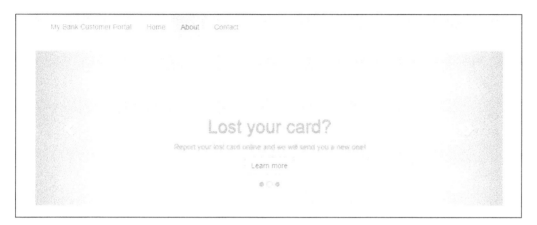

We have reached our second checkpoint. The code for this checkpoint can be found at `chapter5\checkpoint2`.

Viewing accounts

We will implement the third user story in this section, which is about displaying account information to the members of MyBank. The requirements for this story, as mandated by the client, are that the account information be displayed in a table under the accounts tab that we created earlier. The account information must include the name of the branch the account is held at, the account number, type of account, and the current account balance. The accounts in the table should also be numbered. The client has also stated that any amount figure displayed in the application should be in the currency format.

This story requires us to retrieve account information from the server side. To keep the implementation simple and to focus on the client-side development, a server stub is provided, which simulates the server interaction. Let's get started by including the stub in our application. Download the `serverstub.js` file from `chapter5\server`. Copy the file to the `javascript` folder of your project. Edit `bankportal.html` and include `serverstub.js` before the JavaScript file for our bank portal module. The JavaScript inclusion should now look similar to this:

```
<script type="text/javascript"
src="javascript/jquery-2.1.3.min.js"></script>
<script type="text/javascript"
src="javascript/knockout-3.2.0.js"></script>
<script type="text/javascript"
src="javascript/knockout.validation.min.js"></script>
<script type="text/javascript"
src="bootstrap/js/bootstrap.min.js"></script>
<script type="text/javascript"
src="javascript/serverstub.js"></script>
<script type="text/javascript"
src="javascript/bankportal.js"></script>
```

The server stub gives us a method called `getMemberData`, which retrieves and returns member data object containing members personal and account information. To use this module, declare an attribute in your bank portal module and execute the server module:

```
/* module to retrieve data from the server */
var server = ServerStub();
```

We can now retrieve the member data by calling the `getMemberData` method. Here is an example:

```
console.log("Retrieving data from server......")
var data = server.getMemberData();
```

The next step is to declare the model and populate it with the data retrieved from the server side. Our model at this stage will only contain an array to hold the accounts. Declare the model like this:

```
/* the model */
var member = {
    accounts: ko.observableArray()
};
```

The data returned by our server is an object, which is an array of accounts. Each account has an object called `summary`, which contains the name of the branch the account is held at, account number, type, and account balance. We will populate our accounts array in the model with the `summary` objects in the data retrieved from the server. Let's do this in a method and call it `retrieveData`. Here is our implementation of this method:

```
/* method retrieves data from the server side and sets it in the
model */
var retrieveData = function() {
  console.log("Retrieving data from server......")
  var data = server.getMemberData();
  console.log("Data retrieved from server: " + ko.toJSON(data));

//add accounts to the model
  data.accounts.forEach(function(account) {
    member.accounts.push({summary: account.summary});
  });
};
```

The method retrieves the member data by calling the `getMemberData` method on the server stub module. It logs the data to the console in the form of JSON string. The `Ko.toJSON` method is used to convert the object to its JSON string representation. The second part of the method iterates over the accounts array in the data and adds the `summary` objects to our accounts' observable array. You can now call this method from the `init` method of the bank portal module:

```
var init = function () {
  /* add code to initialize this module */
  retrieveData();
  //apply ko bindings
  ko.applyBindings(BankPortal);
};
```

Try running the application in the browser and view the console window. You should see the data retrieved printed in the logs. Our **Console** window looks similar to this:

```
Q  [ ]  Elements  Network  Sources  Timeline  Profiles  Resources  Audits | Console |          >≡  ⚙  ☐, ×

⊘  ▽  <top frame>  ▼  ☐ Preserve log

Retrieving data from server......                                                    bankportal.js:44
Data retrieved from server: {"personal":{"firstName":"John","lastName":"Citizen","address":{"street":"1  bankportal.js:46
Main
Street","city":"Melbourne","postCode":3000,"country":"Australia"},"phoneNumber":399998888,"emailAddress":"john.citizen@em
ail.com"},"accounts":[{"summary":{"branch":"Collingwood","number":"0612
30042","type":"Savings","balance":700},"transactions":[{"date":"20 May","description":"Collingwood milk
bar","category":"Grocery","amount":23},{"date":"18 May","description":"Food store","category":"Food","amount":13},
{"date":"15 April","description":"Collingwood milk bar","category":"Grocery","amount":53},{"date":"12
March","description":"Sushi shop","category":"Food","amount":28}]},{"summary":{"branch":"Clayton","number":"0652
20172","type":"Savings","balance":313.64},"transactions":[{"date":"21 May","description":"Clayton milk
bar","category":"Grocery","amount":63},{"date":"19 May","description":"No 8 Southbank","category":"Food","amount":450},
{"date":"13 April","description":"State library","category":"Work","amount":53},{"date":"11 March","description":"Bags
for sale","category":"Shopping","amount":78}]},{"summary":{"branch":"Mitcham","number":"0682
40742","type":"Credit","balance":60000},"transactions":[{"date":"23 June","description":"Black coder
coffee","category":"Food","amount":53},{"date":"21 May","description":"Food store","category":"Grocery","amount":63},
{"date":"13 April","description":"Money transfer","category":"Transfer","amount":500},{"date":"09
March","description":"Sushi shop","category":"Food","amount":68},{"date":"08
March","description":"Donuts","category":"Food","amount":50}]},{"summary":{"branch":"Doncaster","number":"0612
40772","type":"Cheque","balance":10000},"transactions":[]}]}
> |
```

One last step we must perform on the module, before we can start on the view, is to create a strategy to display the amount in currency format. We have a few options on how to achieve this. We can iterate over the accounts and convert each amount attribute into a formatted currency string. Another option is to add a computed observable that returns the formatted amount. Using extenders is also an option. However, a more generic solution is to construct a custom binding that returns a given number to a formatted currency string.

A custom binding is created by adding a binding handler to Knockout binding handler object. Here is the basic construct:

```
ko.bindingHandlers.customBindingName = {
    init: function(element, valueAccessor) {
        // called when binding is first applied to the element
    },
    update: function(element, valueAccessor) {
        // called when binding is first applied and every time the
        observable changes value
    }
};
```

The `init` method is called when the binding is first applied to the DOM element. The `update` method is called when the binding is first applied and every time the observable changes its value. The `element` parameter in the two method is the underlying DOM element. The `valueAccessor` is a function that returns the current value of the property in the model. We apply the custom binding just like any other binding:

```
<div data-bind="customBindingName: attributeValue"> </div>
```

Let's use the custom bind construct described here to create a custom binding that formats our account balance from a number to a formatted currency text. I recommend creating a separate module for defining all the Knockout customizations. Create a module in its own JavaScript file. We will call the file, `configureknockout.js`, and the module, `ConfigureKnockout`. Include the newly created JavaScript file in `bankportal.html`. The `include` statement for `configureknockout.js` must be after the core Knockout JavaScript file and before `bankportal.js`. The module does not need to return anything in its `return` statement as it does not contain any attributes or function that need to accessed publically. Now, add a custom binding handler that accesses the value of the observable, formats the value as a currency string, and sets the formatted string in the DOM element. Our implementation of the module looks similar to this:

```
/* Module for configuring Knockout */
var ConfigureKnockout = function () {

  /* method to add custom currency binding */
  var applyCurrencyBinding = function () {
    /* custom binding for currency */
    ko.bindingHandlers.currency = {
      update: function(element, valueAccessor){
        // retrieve observable value
        var value = ko.utils.unwrapObservable(valueAccessor()) ||
        0;
            //format currency
        var formattedText =  "$" +
        value.toFixed(2).replace(/(\d)(?=(\d{3})+\.)/g, "$1,");
        //apply formatted text to the underlying DOM element
        $(element).text(formattedText);
      }
    };
  };

  /* add code to initialize this module */
  var init = function () {
```

```
        applyCurrencyBinding();
    }();

    return {
        /* nothing to return */
    };
}();
```

The module has an `applyCurrencyBinding` method, which is called from the `init` method. Notice that the `init` method is fired when the module is loaded. It does not have to wait for the HTML document to be ready. It does have a dependency on Knockout and must be loaded after the core Knockout library. The `applyCurrencyBinding` method creates the custom currency handler, `ko.bindingHandlers.currency`. The currency handler has a method called `update`. The `update` method retrieves the value of our observable by calling the `valueAccessor` method. It unwraps the observable to its plain value by using `ko.utils.unwrapObservable`. The value is set to `0` if no value is returned by the observable. The value is then formatted to a currency text by using a regex expression. The last step is to set the value in the underlying DOM element. We use jQuery to set the text value in the DOM element.

Now that we have retrieved data from the server side, populated our model, and created a custom binding to display currency, we can work on the view. Open the view in `bankportal.html` and locate the `div` element for accounts. The `div` element should have `id="accounts"` and its contents should be `<p>--- Content for Accounts goes here ---</p>`. Delete the current contents and replace it with a table. Use the `foreach` binding to render the accounts from the model. The table should have columns for row number, branch name, account number, account type, and account balance. Use currency custom binding for the account balance. We can use `$index()` to display the row number by adding one to it. The rest of the columns map to the attributes in the `account` object of our model. Wrap the table in a panel and give it a heading. Make the component responsive by wrapping it in `div` and giving it the `row` and `col-md-12` style classes. Use `table-hover` style class on the `table` element to give its rows a hover effect. Our implementation looks similar to this:

```html
<div id="accounts" data-bind="visible:
BankPortal.isActiveTab('Accounts')">
  <div class="row">
    <div class="col-md-12">
      <div class="panel panel-default">
        <div class="panel-heading">Summary</div>
```

```
        <div class="panel-body">
          <table class="table table-hover">
            <thead>
              <tr>
                <th>#</th>
                <th>Branch</th>
                <th>Number</th>
                <th>Type</th>
                <th>Balance</th>
              </tr>
            </thead>
            <tbody data-bind="foreach:
            BankPortal.member.accounts">
              <tr>
                <td data-bind="text: ($index() + 1)"></td>
                <td data-bind="text: summary.branch"></td>
                <td data-bind="text: summary.number"></td>
                <td data-bind="text: summary.type"></td>
                <td data-bind="currency: summary.balance"></td>
              </tr>
            </tbody>
          </table>
        </div>
      </div>
    </div>
  </div>
</div>
```

As you may have noticed, we have used the Bootstrap panel to give our table a header. The header is in the `div` element with the `panel-heading` style class. The table is wrapped in the `div` with the `panel-body` style class.

Try running the application in your browser. You should see the table with the account information retrieved from the server. Move the mouse over the rows to see the hover effect. In our browser, it looks similar to the following screenshot:

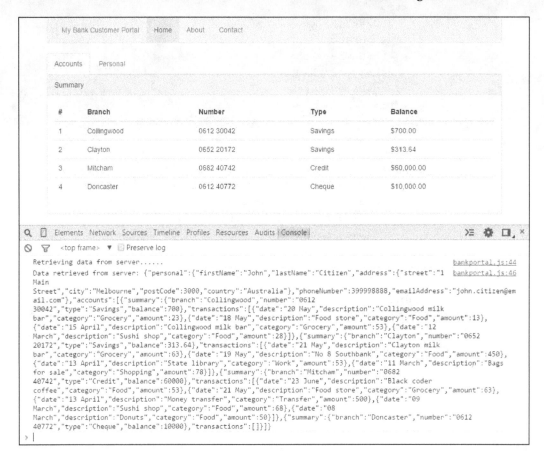

We have reached our third checkpoint. The code for this checkpoint can be found at chapter5\checkpoint3.

Viewing transactions for an account

The next user story is about displaying transactions made for an account. The client wants to see the transactions listed in a table below the accounts table we developed in the previous section. The user must be able to select the account by clicking on the row to view the account's transactions. A transaction must include the date the transaction took place, a short description of the transaction, transaction category, and the amount. The transactions in the table should also be numbered. The user should be informed to select an account to see transaction and if no transactions exist for an account.

The transactions data for each account is retrieved from the sever side as part of the `server.getMemberData` call. Each account object in the returned data contains a summary and a transactions object. The transactions object is an array of transactions with transaction date, description, category, and amount.

The first step is to allow the user to be able to select an account by clicking on a row in the accounts table. To do this, we will add a click binding on the accounts table row. Add a click binding to the accounts table `tr` element and bind it to the method called `setSelectedAccount` in the `BankPortal` module. The accounts table `tr` element should now look similar to this:

```
<tr data-bind="click: BankPortal.setSelectedAccount">
    ...................
</tr>
```

Let's now add the `setSelectedAccount` method to our module. This method should take one argument—the account that the user clicked on.

 The `click` bind passes the current array object as the first parameter in the bounded method when used within a `foreach` construct.

Update the model to add an attribute to hold our selected account. Set the selected account in the `setSelectedAccount` method. Add the `setSelectedAccount` method to the `return` statement of the module as it is used in the view by the click binding. Our implementation of the `setSelectedAccount` method looks similar to this:

```
/* sets the selected account */
var setSelectedAccount = function (account) {
  console.log("Setting selected account: " +
  account.summary.number);
  member.selectedAccount(account);
};
```

Notice how the selected account is set in the member model. This is because the selected account is an observable and is declared in the model like this:

```
selectedAccount: ko.observable()
```

Now that we know which account the user has selected, it's time to highlight the view. We do this by adding a style called `active` on the selected account. To do this, add a `css` binding to the account table `tr` element and bind it to `isSelectedAccount` method in our module. Pass the current account by passing the `$data` parameter to the method. Unlike the `click` binding, the `css` binding does not pass the current row object by default. Our `tr` element now looks similar to this:

```
<tr data-bind="click: BankPortal.setSelectedAccount, css: {active:
BankPortal.isSelectedAccount($data)}">
```

Update the module to add the `isSelectedAccount` method. This method simply returns either a true or a false by comparing the account passed as the parameter with our selected account from the model. Add the `isSelectedAccount` method to the `return` statement of the module. The implementation should look similar to this:

```
/* returns true if the account matches selected account, false
otherwise */
var isSelectedAccount = function (account) {
  return account === member.selectedAccount();
};
```

Open the application in the browser and try selecting an account by clicking on a row in the accounts table. You should be able to see the selected account highlighted. You should also see the selected account in the console logs. In our browser, it looks similar to the following screenshot; notice how the selected account is highlighted:

The next step is to display the transaction for the selected account. To achieve this, we will add an observable array to the model to hold the selected account's transactions. We will set this observable array with the transactions of the selected account in the `setSelectedAccount` method. We will also update the `retrieveData` method to add an observable array for the account's transactions.

Let's update the `retrieveData` method. We need to add an observable array to the accounts object to hold the account's transactions. The construct to push the accounts to our accounts array in the `retrieveData` method should now look similar to this:

```
//add accounts to the model
data.accounts.forEach(function(account) {
  member.accounts.push({summary: account.summary, transactions:
ko.observableArray(account.transactions)});
});
```

Add a transactions observable array to the model that will be used to hold the transaction for the selected account. Your model should now look similar to this:

```
/* the model */
var member = {
    accounts: ko.observableArray(),
    selectedAccount: ko.observable(),
    selectedAccountTransactions: ko.observableArray([])
};
```

Now we can update our `setSelectedAccount` method to set the transactions for the selected account. Add the transactions from the selected account to the `selectedAccountTransactions` attribute in the model. Our updated `setSelectedAccount` method looks similar to this:

```
/* sets the selected account */
var setSelectedAccount = function (account) {
  console.log("Setting selected account: " +
  account.summary.number);
  member.selectedAccount(account);
  member.selectedAccountTransactions(account.transactions());
};
```

Now that we have populated our model with the transactions and set the selected account, we can now work on the view. Open the view in `bankportal.html` and locate the `div` element for accounts. The `div` should have `id="accounts"`. Add another `div` below the accounts table to display the transactions. Use `foreach` binding to render the `selectedAccountTransactions` function from the model. The table should have columns for row number, date, description, category, and amount. Use currency custom binding for the transaction amount. Use `$index()` to display the row number by adding one to it. Wrap the table in a panel and give it a heading. Make the component responsive by wrapping it in DIV and giving it the `row` and `col-md-12` style classes. Our implementation looks similar to this:

```
<div class="col-md-12">
  <div class="panel panel-default">
```

```
<div class="panel-heading">Transactions</div>
<div class="panel-body">
  <table class="table">
    <thead>
      <tr>
        <th>#</th>
        <th>Date</th>
        <th>Description</th>
        <th>Category</th>
        <th>Amount</th>
      </tr>
    </thead>
    <tbody data-bind="foreach:
    BankPortal.member.selectedAccountTransactions">
      <tr>
        <td data-bind="text: ($index() + 1)"></td>
        <td data-bind="text: date"></td>
        <td data-bind="text: description"></td>
        <td data-bind="text: category"></td>
        <td data-bind="currency: amount"></td>
      </tr>
    </tbody>
  </table>
</div>
</div>
</div>
```

Try running the application in the browser. You should see a panel with a heading, Transactions, under the accounts panel with a table. The table will not have any rows to start with. Try clicking on an account to see the transactions appear. Try switching to another account.

One last step before we can consider this user story done is to inform the user to select an account to see the transactions. The use should also be informed if no transactions exist for an account. We will use the `if` and `ifnot` bindings to achieve this.

 The `if` binding adds the contents to the DOM of the HTML element it is applied to if the condition specified evaluates to true. The `ifnot` binding just inverts the specified condition.

Add a p HTML element before the transactions table with text that informs the user to select an account to view its transactions. Apply the ifnot binding with a condition checking for the selectedAccount method in our model. It should look similar to this:

```
<p data-bind="ifnot: BankPortal.member.selectedAccount">Select an
account to view transactions</p>
```

Add another p HTML with text, informing the user that the account selected does not have any transactions. Apply the if binding with the condition that selectedAccount exists and that the selectedAccount has transactions. It should look similar to this:

```
<p data-bind="if: (BankPortal.member.selectedAccount() &&
BankPortal.member.selectedAccountTransactions().length == 0)">No
transaction exist for this account</p>
```

Notice the use of the && logical operator to construct a more complex expression. Finally, apply the if binding to the transactions table and specify the condition that an account is selected and it has one or more transactions. The table start element with the if condition should look similar to this:

```
<table class="table" data-bind="if:
(BankPortal.member.selectedAccount() &&
BankPortal.member.selectedAccountTransactions().length > 0)">
```

>
> The if and visible bindings play a similar role. The if binding adds or removes the contents of the element it is applied to, whereas the visible binding shows or hides the content using CSS. Use the visible binding if you want the contents in the DOM added but just hidden form the user.

Try running the application in your browser. You should see the table with the account information retrieved from the server with a panel below for transactions. The panel should inform the user to select an account. Try selecting an account to see its transactions. Try looking for an account with no transactions. In our browser, it looks similar to the following screenshot:

We have reached our fourth checkpoint. The code for this checkpoint can be found at `chapter5\checkpoint4`.

Viewing personal information

The last user story for this chapter is about displaying the personal information to the user. The personal information includes user's first name, last name, phone number, e-mail address, and postal address. We are instructed to display this information in a form. The user should not be able to edit the information in the form. The user story to be able to edit the personal information will come at a later stage.

Let's start by retrieving the personal information form the server data and constructing our model. The data for personal information is retrieved from the sever side as part of the `server.getMemberData` call. We need to extract this data and set it in our model. Update the model and add attributes for first name, last name, phone number, e-mail address, and postal address. The postal address should include attributes for street, city, post code, and country. We will make this attributes as observables keeping in mind that we will need to implement the edit functionality in the future. Go ahead and update the model. With the added fields, the model should look similar to this:

```
/* the model */
var member = {
    personal: {
        firstName: ko.observable(),
        lastName: ko.observable(),
        address: {
            street: ko.observable(),
            city: ko.observable(),
            postCode: ko.observable(),
            country: ko.observable()
        },
        contactDetails: {
            phoneNumber: ko.observable(),
            emailAddress: ko.observable()
        }
    },
    accounts: ko.observableArray(),
    selectedAccount: ko.observable(),
    selectedAccountTransactions: ko.observableArray([]),
};
```

Now that we have updated the model, let's populate it with the data from the server side. Update the `retrieveData` method to add code for populating the model. Our `retrieveData` method should now look similar to this:

```
/* method retrieves data from the server side and sets it in the
model */
var retrieveData = function() {
  console.log("Retrieving data from server......")
  var data = server.getMemberData();
  console.log("Data retrieved from server: " + ko.toJSON(data));

  //add accounts to the model
  data.accounts.forEach(function(account) {
    member.accounts.push({summary: account.summary, transactions:
    ko.observableArray(account.transactions)});
  });

  //add personal information to the model
  member.personal.firstName(data.personal.firstName);
  member.personal.lastName(data.personal.lastName);
  member.personal.contactDetails.phoneNumber(data.personal.
  phoneNumber);
  member.personal.contactDetails.emailAddress(data.personal.
  emailAddress);

  member.personal.address.street(data.personal.address.street);
  member.personal.address.city(data.personal.address.city);
  member.personal.address.postCode(data.personal.address.postCode);
  member.personal.address.country(data.personal.address.country);
};
```

Now that our model is ready, we can work on the view. Open the view in `bankportal.html` and locate the `div` element for personal. The `div` element should have `id="personal"` and its contents should be `<p>--- Content for Personal goes here ---</p>`. Delete the place holder `p` element and use a panel for personal information with a panel header and a body, similar to the panel we used for the accounts. Use a form to display the personal information. Bind the form input elements to the observables in the model. Mark the input fields as read only by using the `enable` binding. Let's start with first name, last name, phone number, and e-mail address. So far, our form looks similar to this:

```
<form>
  <fieldset>
    <div class="row">
      <div class="col-md-6">
```

```
            <div class="form-group">
              <label for="firstNameInput">First Name</label>
              <input type="text" class="form-control"
              data-bind="enable: false, value:
              BankPortal.member.personal.firstName"
              id="firstNameInput">
            </div>
          </div>
          <div class="col-md-6">
            <div class="form-group">
              <label for="lastNameInput">Last Name</label>
              <input type="text" class="form-control"
              data-bind="enable: false, value:
              BankPortal.member.personal.lastName" id="lastNameInput">
            </div>
          </div>
        </div>
        <div class="row">
          <div class="col-md-6">
            <div class="form-group">
              <label for="phoneNumberInput">Phone number</label>
              <input type="text" class="form-control"
              data-bind="enable: false, value:
              BankPortal.member.personal.contactDetails.phoneNumber"
              id="phoneNumberInput">
            </div>
          </div>
          <div class="col-md-6">
            <div class="form-group">
              <label for="emailInput">Email</label>
              <input type="text" class="form-control"
              data-bind="enable: false, value:
              BankPortal.member.personal.contactDetails.emailAddress"
              id="emailInput">
            </div>
          </div>
        </div>
      </fieldset>
    </form>
```

Try running the application in the browser and view the personal tab. You should see the form with the fields we created using the preceding code. Notice that the fields are read only. This is because we used the enable binding on the input fields and specified it as false.

Complete the form by adding the fields for postal address details. Run the application again once you have added the fields for the address. You should now see all the fields under the personal tab. In our browser, it should look similar to the following screenshot:

We have reached our last checkpoint for this chapter. The code for this checkpoint can be found at `chapter5\checkpoint5`.

Summary

In this chapter, we walked through building a customer banking portal for MyBank. We took an iterative approach to develop the application as instructed by the CIO of MyBank.

In the first section, we implemented a user story that was about setting up the navigation so that the users could easily navigate through the application and find the information they require. We developed a navigation bar and a tab container to display different sections of the view. The second section was about displaying static information on different view sections. We developed a carousel component to display useful information and also learned how to use the panels. We implemented the displaying of accounts information in the third section of the chapter. We retrieved user data from the server and mapped it to our model. The fourth section was about giving our users the ability to select an account and view its transactions. We achieved this by developing a master details component using tables. In the last section, we implemented displaying user information in a form.

In the next chapter, we will enhance the customer banking portal by adding new features. We will give our users the ability to edit their personal information and transfer funds between their accounts.

6
Enhancing the Customer Banking Portal

The customer banking portal we developed in the previous chapter was well received by the stockholders at MyBank and the client has decided to enhance the portal by adding more features. The CIO of MyBank wants us to continue with the iterative approach and has given us the following user stories to implement for the second release:

- As a member, I want to be able to update my personal information
- As a member, I want to be able to cancel updating personal information and revert my changes
- As a member, I want to only update validated personal information
- As a member, I want to transfer funds between my accounts

This chapter is the second in the series on building a customer banking portal. It picks up the development from where we left it in the previous chapter and adds new features to it. In this chapter, we will build on the concepts we have learned so far and apply them in constructing more complex components such as wizards, dialog boxes, and sliders.

In this chapter, we will learn how to:

- Enable and disable form fields
- Submit information from a web form to the server side
- Revert changes to observables using the memento pattern
- Validate form fields

- Construct a generic and reusable wizard component
- Communicate events between modules using call backs
- Use the wizard component to develop business features

As mandated by the CIO of MyBank, we will continue taking the iterative approach to building the application. Each user story or feature has a corresponding checkpoint folder in the accompanying code.

Updating personal information

The last story of the previous chapter was about displaying the personal information to the user. The personal information included user's first name, last name, phone number, e-mail address, and postal address. This story builds on where we left the application in the previous chapter and gives the users the ability to update their personal information.

We implemented a form with its input fields disabled for displaying the personal information. The requirements for this user story are to allow the user to enable the form fields so that the information can be updated. The fields should go back to disabled state once the personal information is updated. The user should also be informed when the personal information fields are updated on the server.

You should start on this story by checking out code from `chapter5\checkpoint5`. This story requires an updated server stub. Download the `serverstub.js` file from `chapter6\server`. Copy the `serverstub.js` file to the `javascript` folder of your project, overriding the existing `serverstub.js` file. Run the application by opening the `bankportal.html` file in the browser. Do a quick sanity check of the application by making sure that the features we implemented in the previous chapter are functional. We are now ready to develop the user story for updating personal information.

We will use an attribute to specify whether the form fields are editable or not. Let's call this attribute `personalInformationEditMode`. This attribute must be an observable as we will use it to enable or disable form fields. Open the module in the `bankportal.js` file and add this attribute:

```
/* edit mode for personal information */
var personalInformationEditMode = ko.observable(false);
```

Add the preceding attribute to the `return` statement of the module so that it becomes accessible from the view. We need a method to enable edit mode for personal information form fields by setting `personalInformationEditMode` to `true` and a method to disable the edit mode by setting the attribute to `false`. Add these two methods to the module. Our implementation of these methods could look similar to this:

```
/* method to enable personal information edit mode */
var enablePersonalnformationEdit = function () {
  personalInformationEditMode(true);
};
/* method to cancel personal information edit mode */
var cancelPersonalInformationEdit = function () {
  personalInformationEditMode(false);
};
```

The next step is to add a method to submit the personal information to the server side. The server stub exposes a method called `updatePersonalInformation`, which we will use to send the personal information to the server side. This method takes an object as the parameter that holds the personal information. We will need to convert our model, holding the personal information, from an observable to a plain JavaScript object to pass it to the `updatePersonalInformation` method. To do this, we use the `ko.toJS` method. Given an observable, this method returns a plain JavaScript object. Our implementation of the method looks similar to this:

```
/* method to submit personal information to the server */
var submitPersonalInformation = function () {
  console.log("Updating personal information on the server: " +
  ko.toJSON(member.personal));
  server.updatePersonalInformation(ko.toJS(member.personal));
  console.log("Personal information updated on the server.....")

  personalInformationEditMode(false);
};
```

 The `ko.toJS` method returns a plain copy of the view model that only contains the data without any Knockout-related artifacts. It returns a JSON string representation of the view model.

Notice the use of `ko.toJS` method. Also note that we are setting the edit mode of the personal information form fields to `false` once we have updated the personal information. Don't forget to add this and the two methods we created earlier in this session to the `return` statement of the module so that they become publically accessible.

We are now ready to start on the view. We will add a button after the form fields to enable edit mode. Add this button before the closing `form` HTML element of the personal information form and give it a label. Add a click binding to the button and bind it to the `enablePersonalnformationEdit` method of the module. The button should only appear if the edit mode for personal information in not enabled. Add a visible binding to the button and check for `personalInformationEditMode`. The button should look similar to this:

```
<button type="button" class="btn btn-default" data-bind="visible:
BankPortal.personalInformationEditMode() == false, click:
BankPortal.enablePersonalnformationEdit">Edit</button>
```

 Knockout bindings automatically unwrap observables and use their value. If there were an invisible binding, we would not need to unwrap the `personalInformatioEditMode` observable used in the preceding code.

The next step is to make the form fields enable or disable based on the edit mode. Do this by updating the `enable` data binding to check for `personalInformationEditMode`. The following is an example for the first name field with the change highlighted:

```
<div class="form-group">
  <label for="firstNameInput">First Name</label>
  <input type="text" class="form-control" data-bind="enable:
  BankPortal.personalInformationEditMode, value:
  BankPortal.member.personal.firstName" id="firstNameInput">
</div>
```

Update the rest of the form fields and apply the enable binding with `personalInformationEditMode`. We can add the `Submit` button now so that we can enable the form fields for editing. Add a button of type `submit` under the previously added **Edit** button. Add a `visible` binding to this button and make it appear only if the `edit` mode is enabled. It should look similar to this:

```
<button type="submit" class="btn btn-primary" data-bind="visible:
BankPortal.personalInformationEditMode">Submit</button>
```

We now add a `submit` binding to the form and specify the method to be called in our module when the **Submit** button is clicked. Add the `submit` binding to the form and specify the `submitPersonalInformation` method in our module. The form should look similar to the following example; note that the form body is not shown:

```
<div class="panel panel-default">
  <div class="panel-heading">Personal Information</div>
  <div class="panel-body">
```

```
      <form data-bind="submit:
      BankPortal.submitPersonalInformation">
        <fieldset>
          ... ... ...
        </fieldset>
      </form>
    </div>
  </div>
```

Open the application in your browser. Go to the personal information tab under the home navigation page. You should now see a button, under the form, labeled **Edit**. Clicking this button should enable the `edit` mode. You should now see a button labeled **Submit**. The form fields should also become editable. Try updating the personal information and hit the **Submit** button. The updated data should get sent to the server side and the form should exit the edit mode.

The last step in this story is to inform the user once the personal information has been updated on the server side. We will use a Bootstrap alert construct to display a message to the user. The message will get displayed based on a flag in the module. A flag is just an attribute that is used to indicate a state. We will call this flag `showPersonalInformationEditDone`. Open the view and add the alert as the first element after the `form` element. Make the alert appear based on the `showPersonalInformationEditDone` flag in the module by using the `visible` binding. It should look similar to this:

```
  <div class="panel panel-default">
    <div class="panel-heading">Personal Information</div>
    <div class="panel-body">
      <form data-bind="submit:
      BankPortal.submitPersonalInformation">
        <div class="alert alert-success" role="alert"
        data-bind="visible:
        BankPortal.showPersonalInformationEditDone">
        <strong>Done! </strong>Personal information updated </div>
        <fieldset>
          ... ... ...
        </fieldset>
      </form>
    </div>
  </div>
```

Update the module to add the `showPersonalInformationEditDone` flag. Add the flag to the `return` statement of the module. It should look similar to this:

```
/* flag to show personal information update message */
var showPersonalInformationEditDone = ko.observable(false);
```

Note that the flag is initially set to `false`. Set the flag to `true` in the `submitPersonalInformation` method. Set the flag to `false` in the `enablePersonalnformationEdit` method.

Open the application in the browser. Navigate to the **Personal Information** tab and try enabling the `edit` mode. Update the information in the form fields and hit **Submit**. You should see the updated information sent to the server. The form should come out of the `edit` mode and you should see a message informing you that the personal information has been updated. In our browser, this feature looks similar to this:

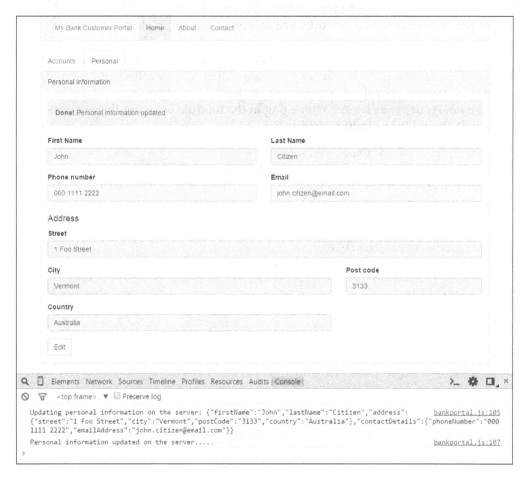

We have reached our first checkpoint for this chapter. The code for this checkpoint can be found at `chapter6\checkpoint1`.

Cancel updating the personal information

We gave our users the ability to edit their personal information in the previous user story. Once the users start editing, they do not have a way to cancel if they don't want to go ahead with the changes. In this user story, we will give our users the ability to cancel editing the personal information form. The requirement of the user story is to provide a button, with a label **Cancel**, in the `edit` mode. Clicking the **Cancel** button should revert any changes made to the form fields and take the form out of the `edit` mode. The user would also like to be informed that the edit was cancelled and any change to personal information was not saved.

Let's start by adding the **Cancel** button to the view. Add a button under the **Submit** button of the personal form. Give the button a label of **Cancel**. The button should only be displayed if the personal information form is in the `edit` mode. Add a `visible` binding to the button to make it appear only in the `edit` mode, similar to the `edit` button. Add a `click` binding to the button and bind it to the `cancelPersonalInformationEdit` method. The code should look similar to this:

```
<button type="button" class="btn btn-default" data-bind="visible:
BankPortal.personalInformationEditMode, click:
BankPortal.cancelPersonalInformationEdit">Cancel</button>
```

The next step is to add the `cancelPersonalInformationEdit` method to the module. Open the module in the `bankportal.js` file. Define the `cancelPersonalInformationEdit` method and add it to the `return` statement of the module. The `cancelPersonalInformationEdit` method should make the personal information form exit the `edit` mode by setting the mode to `false`. Our implementation looks similar to this:

```
/* method to cancel personal information edit mode */
var cancelPersonalInformationEdit = function () {
  personalInformationEditMode(false);
};
```

Run the application in the browser. Go to the **Personal Information** form and click on the **Edit** button. The **Cancel** button should appear next to the **Submit** button. Edit the information in the form fields and click on **Cancel** to exit the `edit` mode. Notice that the edited information in the form fields is retained after the **Cancel** button is clicked upon. The edited information is not submitted to the server, but due to the two-way binding, the values of observables are updated as soon as the data is modified in the `form` fields. In our scenario, we would like to give the users the ability to accept or cancel their edits. We have a few different options to achieve this.

One option is to reload the data from the server side if users cancel their edits. The downside of this approach is the overhead of retrieving the data from the server. The edits made by the user might be in a subset of the data (this is the case in our scenario). We do not want to pull a fresh set of account and transaction information every time the user clicks on **Cancel** on the personal information form.

Another option is to save a copy of the data retrieved as part of the initial call to the server. On cancel, we can simply reinitialize the observables for personal information with the data we saved. This is simple and works as well, but it requires holding a copy of the server-side data, which will need to be updated or kept in sync every time any data is submitted to the server.

We could have temporary observables for the fields we want to make editable. The value in these temporary observables could be reinitialized if the user decides to cancel. On submit, the data from these temporary observables could be copied to the real observables. This approach works well, but it requires copying values between the temporary and real observables.

The option, which I recommend and will use to solve this issue, is the use of custom observables that implement the **memento design pattern**.

 The memento design pattern captures the internal state of an object and provides the ability to restore the object to its previous state when required. You can read more about the memento design pattern in the book, *Design Patterns: Elements of Reusable Object-Oriented Software*.

Let's create the custom observable. We will call it `mementoObservable`. Open the module in the `configureknockout.js` file. Add a method to create the observable. We will call this method `createMementoObservable`. The method should declare the observable called `mementoObservable`. The observable is a function that encapsulates a normal observable to hold the current state of the object. The function also encapsulates the memento or the previous state of the object. The observable, `mementoObservable`, should also expose two methods—one to reset the object to its memento state and another to commit the current state to the memento state. Our implementation of `mementoObservable` looks similar to this:

```
/* method to add memento observable */
var createMementoObservable = function () {
  /* memento custom observable */
  ko.mementoObservable = function(initialValue) {
    //the current state
    var state = ko.observable(initialValue);
    //the remembered state
    var mementoState = initialValue;
    //commit the state
    state.commit = function() {
      mementoState = state();
    };
    //reset state from memory
    state.reset = function() {
      state(mementoState);
    };
    //return the current state
    return state;
  };
};
```

Note that, on initialization, the value for state and memento is the same. We use the `state` observable to bind with the input fields. The value of the `state` observable will change as the user edits the form. We will call the `reset` method to revert the user changes to the previously committed value by reinitializing the value of the state observable with memento state. We will call the `commit` method when the user wants to submit their changes.

We are now ready to modify our application to use the `mementoObservable`. Open the bank portal module and change the observables for personal information in the model to use the memento observable. The model should now look similar to this:

```
/* the model */
var member = {
    personal: {
        firstName: ko.mementoObservable(),
        lastName: ko.mementoObservable(),
        address: {
            street: ko.mementoObservable(),
            city: ko.mementoObservable(),
            postCode: ko.mementoObservable(),
            country: ko.mementoObservable()
        },
        contactDetails: {
            phoneNumber: ko.mementoObservable(),
            emailAddress: ko.mementoObservable()
        }
    },
    accounts: ko.observableArray(),
    selectedAccount: ko.observable(),
    selectedAccountTransactions: ko.observableArray([]),
};
```

The next step is to add the methods to commit the state and reset the state of all the memento observables. We will call these methods when the user submits or cancels the edit. Our implementation of a method to commit the state of all the memento observables looks similar to this;. I have called this method `commitPersonalInformation`:

```
/* method to commit state of personal information memento
observables */
var commitPersonalInformation = function () {
    member.personal.firstName.commit();
    member.personal.lastName.commit();
    member.personal.contactDetails.phoneNumber.commit();
    member.personal.contactDetails.emailAddress.commit();
    member.personal.address.street.commit();
    member.personal.address.city.commit();
    member.personal.address.postCode.commit();
    member.personal.address.country.commit();
};
```

Add a method to reset the state of all the memento observables, similar to the `commit` method here. Call this method `resetPersonalInformation`. Our implementation looks similar to this:

```
/* method to reset state of personal information memento
observables */
var resetPersonalInformation = function () {
  member.personal.firstName.reset();
  member.personal.lastName.reset();
  member.personal.contactDetails.phoneNumber.reset();
  member.personal.contactDetails.emailAddress.reset();
  member.personal.address.street.reset();
  member.personal.address.city.reset();
  member.personal.address.postCode.reset();
  member.personal.address.country.reset();
};
```

Modify the `cancelPersonalInformationEdit` method and add a call to reset the value of personal information observables:

```
/* method to cancel personal information edit mode */
var cancelPersonalInformationEdit = function () {
  console.log("Cancelled edit personal information, values
  reverted.....");
personalInformationEditMode(false);
  resetPersonalInformation();
};
```

Modify the `submitPersonalInformation` method to commit the state of personal information observables before the model is submitted to the server. Here is the updated `submitPersonalInformation` method:

```
/* method to submit personal information to the server */
var submitPersonalInformation = function () {
  //commit the state of personal information observables
  commitPersonalInformation();

  console.log("Updating personal information on the server: " +
  ko.toJSON(member.personal));
  server.updatePersonalInformation(ko.toJS(member.personal));
  console.log("Personal information updated on the server.....")

  //switch off the edit mode
  personalInformationEditMode(false);
  //show message that the submit was successful
  showPersonalInformationEditDone(true);
};
```

The last requirement before we can consider this user story done is to inform the user that the edit was cancelled and that any change to the personal information was reverted. We will use a similar approach to the success message we display on successful submit of the personal information to the server. Add a Bootstrap alert construct to display the cancel edit message below the alert construct for the success message. Make the message visible of a showPersonalInformationEditCancel flag. It should look similar to this:

```
<div class="panel panel-default">
  <div class="panel-heading">Personal Information</div>
  <div class="panel-body">
    <form data-bind="submit:
    BankPortal.submitPersonalInformation">
      <div class="alert alert-success" role="alert"
      data-bind="visible:
      BankPortal.showPersonalInformationEditDone">
      <strong>Done! </strong>Personal information updated </div>
      <div class="alert alert-warning" role="alert"
      data-bind="visible:
      BankPortal.showPersonalInformationEditCancel">
      <strong>Cancelled! </strong>Edit cancelled and values reverted
      </div>
      <fieldset>
        ... ... ...
      </fieldset>
    </form>
  </div>
</div>
```

Add the flag to the module with an initial value of false. Don't forget to also add the flag to the return statement of the module. Set the flag to true in the cancelPersonalInformationEdit method. Set the flag to false in the enablePersonalnformationEdit method.

Open the application in the browser after applying the steps described here. Navigate to the personal information form and click on **Edit**. Change the value of some of the form fields and click on **Cancel**. You should now see the message informing you that the edit has been cancelled and the changes have been reverted. In our browser, it looks similar to the following screenshot:

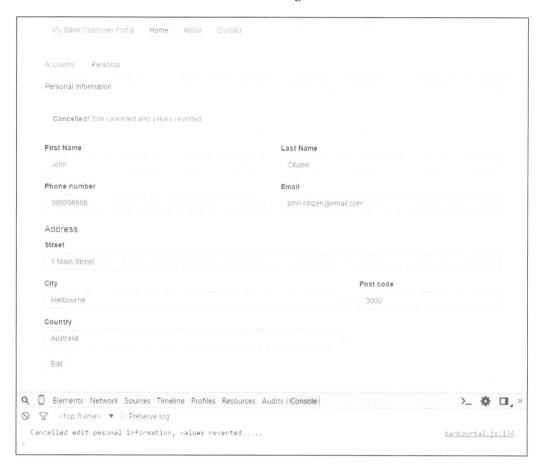

We have reached our second checkpoint of this chapter. The code for this checkpoint can be found at `chapter6\checkpoint2`.

Validating personal information

This user story is about validating that inputs for personal information in the form. The requirements are that all the fields for personal information are valid. In addition, the phone number should be a numeric with a minimum length of four and maximum length of nine. The e-mail should be of a valid e-mail syntax. The post code field for the postal address should be a numeric with a maximum length of four.

We will use the Knockout validation plugin to implement these requirements. You should be familiar with the Knockout validation plugin from *Chapter 4, Adding Validation to the Customer Registration Form*.

Let's start by making sure that we have included the Knockout validation plugin in our application. Open the view in `bankportal.html` and check whether the Knockout validation plugin is included in the HTML head. Download and include the plugin if it is not included already. The HTML head element should look similar to this:

```html
<head>
  <meta http-equiv="Content-Type" content="text/html" />
  <title>Knockout : Customer banking portal</title>

  <link rel="stylesheet" href="bootstrap/css/bootstrap.min.css">
  <link rel="stylesheet" href="css/carousel.css">

  <script type="text/javascript"
  src="javascript/jquery-2.1.3.min.js"></script>
  <script type="text/javascript"
  src="javascript/knockout-3.2.0.js"></script>
  <script type="text/javascript"
  src="javascript/knockout.validation.min.js"></script>
  <script type="text/javascript"
  src="javascript/configureknockout.js"></script>
  <script type="text/javascript"
  src="bootstrap/js/bootstrap.min.js"></script>
  <script type="text/javascript"
  src="javascript/serverstub.js"></script>
  <script type="text/javascript"
  src="javascript/bankportal.js"></script>
</head>
```

The next step is to configure the Knockout validation plugin to work with Bootstrap. Open the module in the `configureknockout.js` file. Add a method called `configureValidationPlugin` and call it from the `init` method of the module. The `init` method should now look similar to this:

```
/* add code to initialize this module */
var init = function () {
  applyCurrencyBinding();
  createMementoObservable();
  configureValidationPlugin();
}();
```

In the body of the `configureValidationPlugin` method, configure the validation to use the Bootstrap classes, `has-error` and `help-block`, for validating error messages. The implementation should look similar to this:

```
var configureValidationPlugin = function () {
  //initialize and configure the validation plugin
  ko.validation.init({
    errorElementClass: 'has-error',
    errorMessageClass: 'help-block'
  });
};
```

We are now ready to start applying validation rules to the observables in the model. Let's first tackle the first name field. Add the required extender to the first name observable in our model. The following is an example of how to apply the required extender to the `firstName` observable:

```
firstName: ko.mementoObservable().extend({ required: true}),
```

We are now ready to modify the view. Open the `bankportal.html` file and locate the first name input field. All we need to do is specify the `validationElement` data binding to the surrounding `div` element. The following is an example of the first name field:

```
<div class="col-md-6" data-bind="validationElement:
BankPortal.member.personal.firstName">
  <div class="form-group">
    <label for="firstNameInput">First Name</label>
    <input type="text" class="form-control" data-bind="enable:
    BankPortal.personalInformationEditMode, value:
    BankPortal.member.personal.firstName" id="firstNameInput">
  </div>
</div>
```

The next step is to capture the errors in a variable so that we can check for the errors when the form gets submitted. To do this, declare a variable in the module; we will call this variable `validationErrors`:

```
/* model validation errors */
var validationErrors;
```

Initialize the `validationErrors` variable with the model in the `init` method:

```
var init = function () {
    /* add code to initialize this module */
    retrieveData();
    //model validation errors
    validationErrors = ko.validation.group(member, { deep: true });
    //apply ko bindings
    ko.applyBindings(BankPortal);
};
```

Now we can check whether any error occurred in the `submitPersonalInformation` method of the module. Do not proceed with submitting the model to the server if validation fails. The following is our implementation of the method; note that the full method implementation is not shown:

```
var submitPersonalInformation = function () {
   //check if validation errors occurred
if (validationErrors().length > 0) {
     console.log("Member model is valid.....");
     return;
   }
   ... ... ...
};
```

Open the application in the browser. Navigate to the personal information form and enter edit mode by clicking on the **Edit** button. Try removing the first name and click on the **Submit** button. You should see the validation error appear for first name. Click on **Cancel** to revert the change and exit edit mode. In our browser, it looks like the following screenshot:

Now that we have validation configured and working for the first name field, we can apply validation to the rest of the fields. Modify the model to add validation extenders to the other observables of the member model. Modify the fields in the view to add the validationElement data binding, similar to how we did this for the first name field. Try opening the application in the browser after applying these changes and triggering validation for fields other than the first name. Then, try clicking on the **Cancel** button to revert the changes and exit the edit mode.

We have reached our third checkpoint for this chapter. The code for this checkpoint can be found at chapter6\checkpoint3.

Transferring funds between accounts

In this user story, we will give the customers of MyBank the ability to transfer funds between their accounts. Our user experience consultant has been working with the client and has come up with a design. The design dictates that the transfer feature should be in its own tab container. The **Transfers** tab should display a wizard component. The wizard component should have three steps, a **Next** and a **Back** button for navigation, and a steps indicator. The first step should capture the accounts the user wants to transfer the funds between. The second step should capture the transfer amount and description. The last step should display the summary of the transfer. The user experience consultant has provided the following wireframe that depicts the user interface:

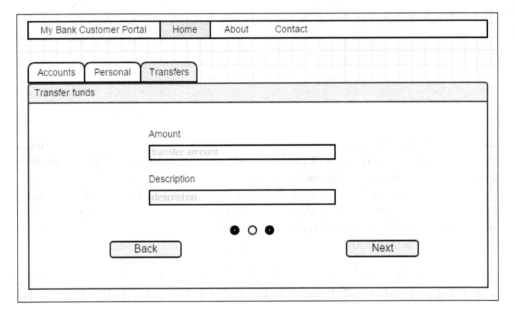

The requirements for this user story has a few different aspects. Let's break the story down and tackle each aspect, one at a time. The first aspect is to create a new tab container for transfer. Once we have our new tab container, we can work on constructing a wizard component. The last aspect is to capture the user input for transfer of funds and submit the request to the server for processing. Let's start with the first aspect.

Creating the Transfers tab

Creating a new tab container is relatively straightforward as we already have two existing tabs — one for accounts and another for personal. To create a new tab container for transfers, open the view in `bankportal.html` and locate the `div` element with the `id="home"` value. The first HTML element of the `div` should be an unordered list with accounts and personal tabs as the list items. Add another list item for transfers, similar to the list items for accounts and personal. The updated list should look similar to this:

```
<ul class="nav nav-tabs">
  <li data-bind="css: {active:
  BankPortal.isActiveTab('Accounts')}">
    <a href="#" data-bind="click:
    BankPortal.setActiveTab.bind($data, 'Accounts')">Accounts</a>
  </li>
  <li data-bind="css: {active:
  BankPortal.isActiveTab('Personal')}">
    <a href="#" data-bind="click:
    BankPortal.setActiveTab.bind($data, 'Personal')">Personal</a>
  </li>
  <li data-bind="css: {active:
  BankPortal.isActiveTab('Transfers')}">
    <a href="#" data-bind="click:
    BankPortal.setActiveTab.bind($data,
    'Transfers')">Transfers</a>
  </li>
</ul>
```

Add a new `div` inside `div` for home page and give it `id="transfers"`. Add a Bootstrap grid and a panel with a heading. Add a placeholder text in the body of the panel for now. We will replace this placeholder text with the wizard component in the next section. Add a visible binding to the `div` and make it appear when **Transfers** is the active tab. Our implementation looks similar to this:

```
<div id="transfers" data-bind="visible:
BankPortal.isActiveTab('Transfers')">
  <div class="row">
    <div class="col-md-12">
      <div class="panel panel-default">
        <div class="panel-heading">Transfer funds</div>
        <div class="panel-body">
          <p> Transfer funds </p>
        </div>
      </div>
    </div>
  </div>
</div>
```

Open the application in the browser. You should see the newly created tab for transfers. Try clicking on the **Transfers** tab to make sure it behaves as expected. It looks similar to the following screenshot in our browser:

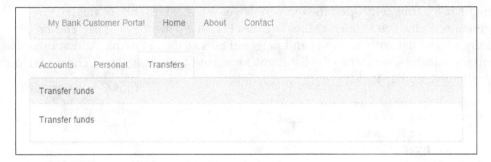

We have reached our fourth checkpoint for this chapter. The code for this checkpoint can be found at `chapter6\checkpoint4`.

Creating the wizard component

The second aspect of this user story is to create a wizard component that will guide the user to transfer funds between accounts. In this section, we will create a generic reusable wizard component. This component will have a module to control the behavior of the wizard component and associated HTML to render the view.

Let's start by creating a module for our wizard. Create a `wizard.js` file in the `javascript` folder and add a blank module using the module pattern. Give the module an appropriate name. I have called it `Wizard`. The module should take number of steps as a parameter. The module should hold, as its state, the number of steps in the wizard and the current step the user is on. We will hold the current step as an observable as it will be used to alter the state of the view. So far, the module should look similar to this:

```
/* Module for Wizard component */
var Wizard = function (steps) {
  /* add members here */
  /* number of steps in the wizard */
```

```
  var numberOfSteps;
  /* current step the wizard is on */
  var currentStep = ko.observable();

/* method to initialize the module */
  var init = function () {
    numberOfSteps = steps;
    currentStep(1);
  };

/* execute the init function */
  init();

  return {
    /* add members that will be exposed publicly */
    currentStep: currentStep
  };
};
```

Notice how the `steps` parameter initializes the `numberOfSteps` attribute of the module. The next step is to include the `wizard.js` file in the `bankportal.html` file. To do this, add the following line to the `head` element of the HTML in the `bankportal.html` file; this should go before the `include` statement of `bankportal.js` file:

```
<script type="text/javascript"
src="javascript/wizard.js"></script>
```

Now we can use the wizard module from the bank portal module. Open the bank portal module in `bankportal.js` and declare a variable for the wizard module. Give it the number of steps for the wizard in our case three. The declaration should look similar to this:

```
/* wizard module for transfer of funds */
var transferWizard = Wizard(3);
```

Add `transferWizard` to the `return` statement of the bank portal module so that we can use it from the view.

Download the `bankportal.css` file from the `chapter6\Checkpoint5\WebContent\css` folder and add it to the `css` folder of your project. This file contains styles for the wizard component. Include the file, as shown here in `bankportal.html`:

```
<link rel="stylesheet" href="css/bankportal.css">
```

We can now start constructing the view for our wizard. Locate the panel we created earlier for transfers under the `div` element with `id="transfers"`. In the panel body, remove the place holder text and add a Bootstrap row with a `row-centered` style class. Add a column with the column width for eight and a style class of `col-centered`. Inside the `div` element for the column, add a `div` element for each of the wizard steps. Apply the `if` binding to these `div` elements to make them appear for the step of the wizard they represent. Add the place holder text in each of the `div` elements. So far, the panel should look similar to this:

```
<div class="panel panel-default">
  <div class="panel-heading">Transfer funds</div>
  <div class="panel-body">
    <div class="row row-centered">
      <div class="col-md-8 col-centered">
        <div class="wizard-step" data-bind="if:
        BankPortal.transferWizard.currentStep() == 1">
          <p> First step</p>
        </div>
        <div class="wizard-step" data-bind="if:
        BankPortal.transferWizard.currentStep() == 2">
          <p> Second step</p>
        </div>
        <div class="wizard-step" data-bind="if:
        BankPortal.transferWizard.currentStep() == 3">
          <p> Third step</p>
        </div>
      </div>
    </div>
  </div>
</div>
```

Notice how the `visible` binding uses the current step of our wizard module. The next step is to add the navigation button to the wizard. Add three buttons under the `div` elements for the steps — two buttons for next and back navigation and one for the last step of the wizard. Label the buttons `Next`, `Back`, and `Done`. Add the `click` bindings to the buttons and bind them to the three corresponding method in the `wizard` module. Add the `visible` bindings to the buttons to make them appear on the appropriate wizard step, that is, the `Next` button should not appear on the last step of the wizard. Similarly the `Back` button should not appear on the first step of the wizard. The `Done` button should only appear on the last step of the wizard. Our implementation of the buttons looks similar to this:

```
<button type="button" class="btn btn-default pull-left"
data-bind="click: BankPortal.transferWizard.back, visible:
BankPortal.transferWizard.isFirstStep() == false">Back</button>
```

```
<button type="button" class="btn btn-primary pull-right"
data-bind="click: BankPortal.transferWizard.next, visible:
BankPortal.transferWizard.isLastStep() == false">Next</button>
<button type="button" class="btn btn-success pull-right"
data-bind="click: BankPortal.transferWizard.done, visible:
BankPortal.transferWizard.isLastStep() == true">Done</button>
```

I have used the `pull-left` and `pull-right` styles provided by Bootstrap to place the buttons to the right and left in the wizard. Notice how I have used the visible binding with the `isFirstStep` and `isLastStep` methods. Next, we will define these methods for the `click` and `visible` binding. Let's tackle the methods for the `click` bindings first. Define the methods—`next`, `back`, and `done`—in the wizard module. The `next` method should increment the current wizard step. Similarly, the `back` method should decrement the current wizard step. The `done` method, for now, should log a message to the console that the user has clicked on the `done` button and reset the wizard to the first step. The implementation to these methods should look similar to this:

```
/* method to go back a step */
var back = function () {
  currentStep(currentStep() - 1);
};

/* method to go forward a step */
var next = function () {
  currentStep(currentStep() + 1);
};

/* method for wizard done */
var done = function () {
  //Done reset wizard and call transfer
  console.log("User clicked done.....");
  currentStep(1);
};
```

The next step is to define the `isFirstStep` and `isLastStep` methods, which are used by the visible bindings on the buttons. These methods should be declared as pure computed observables. They need to be computed observables as they rely on the `currentStep` observable. They should be pure computed as they do not alter the state of the `currentStep` observable. The `isFirstStep` pure computed observable should return `true` if the current wizard step is the first step of the wizard, otherwise, it should return `false`. Similarly, the `isLastStep` pure computed observable should return a `true` if the current step is the last step of the wizard, otherwise, it should return `false`. Create these observables and add them along with the methods for `click` bindings to the return statement of the `wizard` module. Our implementation of these observables should look similar to this:

```
/* returns true if the wizard is on the last step, false otherwise
*/
var isLastStep = ko.pureComputed(function() {
  return currentStep() == numberOfSteps;
});

/* returns true if the wizard is on the first step, false
otherwise */
var isFirstStep = ko.pureComputed(function() {
  return currentStep() == 1;
});
```

Next, we add the step indicators to our wizard component. The step indicators show how many steps the wizard has and indicates the current wizard step. Open the view and locate the buttons for the wizard component. Add an unordered list of HTML element of `ul` with three items—one for each indicator. Give the `ul` element a style class of `wizard-indicators`. Add a `css` binding to the `li` elements and specify the `active` style class based on the current wizard step. Our implementation should look similar to this:

```
<ul class="wizard-indicators">
  <li data-bind="css: { active:
  BankPortal.transferWizard.currentStep() == 1 }"></li>
  <li data-bind="css: { active:
  BankPortal.transferWizard.currentStep() == 2 }"></li>
  <li data-bind="css: { active:
  BankPortal.transferWizard.currentStep() == 3 }"></li>
</ul>
```

Open the application in the browser. Navigate to the tabs for transfers. You should now see the wizard component with a **Next** button and step indicator. Try moving forward and backward in the wizard. Try clicking on the **Done** button. The wizard should look similar to the following screenshot:

We have reached our fifth checkpoint for this chapter. The code for this checkpoint can be found at `chapter6\checkpoint5`.

Adding functionality to the wizard

Now that we have the tab for transfers and the `wizard` component, it's time to add functionality to capture user input and submit a request to the server to transfer funds between two accounts. The requirements state that the first step should capture the accounts the user wants to transfer the funds between. The second step should capture the transfer amount and description. The last step should display the summary of the transfer.

To implement this requirement, we will:

- Add a model to capture the user inputs for fund transfer
- Add input fields on the relevant wizard steps and bind them to the model
- Modify the wizard module to notify the bank portal module when the user has clicked on done
- Submit the transfer of funds request to the sever
- Update the accounts and their transactions in the accounts tab
- Notify the user that the funds have been transferred

Let's get started by adding a model to the bank portal module in `bankportal.js`. This model should capture the accounts for fund transfer, the transfer amount, and the description that should appear in the transaction. Create the model called `transfer` in the bank portal module. Add the model to the `return` statement of the module as we will access it from the view using data binding. The model should look similar to this:

```
/* model for fund transfer */
var transfer = {
  toAccount: ko.observable(),
  fromAccount: ko.observable(),
  amount: ko.observable(),
  description: ko.observable()
};
```

Now, add two dropdowns on the first step of the wizard to capture the accounts the user wants to transfer funds between. Open the view in `bankportal.html` and locate the `div` element for the first wizard step. The `div` element should look similar to this:

```
<div class="wizard-step" data-bind="if:
BankPortal.transferWizard.currentStep() == 1">
... ... ...
</div>
```

Add a row and two columns using the Bootstrap grid. In the first column, add a label for account form and an HTML `select` component. Bind the `select` component to get the options from accounts observable array in the member model. Since the items of the accounts observable array are complex objects, we cannot use them as they are to display the options in the list. We will use the `optionsText` binding to return a string for each item in the accounts observable array. This text is what gets displayed in the list. Use the `optionsText` binding and give it a function that takes the current accounts array item and returns an appropriate text to be displayed in the list. The value of the selected account should be bound to the `fromAccount` attribute of the transfer model. Add a caption to the select component using the `optionsCaption` binding.

Add a column for the account to transfer the funds to, similar to the column for the account to transfer funds from described earlier.

The `optionsCaption` binding adds a dummy option at the beginning of the list and makes it the default option. The value of this dummy option is `undefined`. The dummy option is used to avoid preselecting any option and usually reads "select an option...".

Our implementation of the first wizard step looks similar to this:

```
<div class="wizard-step" data-bind="if:
BankPortal.transferWizard.currentStep() == 1">
  <div class="row row-centered">
    <div class="col-md-8 col-centered">
      <div class="form-group">
        <label class="pull-left" for="accountFrom">Account
        from</label>
        <select id="accountFrom" class="form-control"
            data-bind="options: BankPortal.member.accounts,
                optionsText: function(item) {return
                item.summary.type + ' ' + item.summary.number;},
                optionsCaption: 'Choose from account.....',
                value: BankPortal.transfer.fromAccount">
        </select>
      </div>
    </div>

    <div class="col-md-8 col-centered">
      <div class="form-group">
        <label class="pull-left" for="accountTo">Account
        to</label>
        <select id="accountTo" class="form-control"
            data-bind="options: BankPortal.member.accounts,
                optionsText: function(item) {return
                item.summary.type + ' ' + item.summary.number;},
                optionsCaption: 'Choose to account.....',
                value: BankPortal.transfer.toAccount">
        </select>
      </div>
    </div>
  </div>
</div>
```

Notice the `optionsText` binding. The binding takes a function with the current item of the accounts array as a parameter. I am returning a concatenation of the account type and account number. This string will appear as the option for the given account in the dropdown.

Now, on to the second wizard step, locate the `div` with the second wizard. This `div` should be directly below the `div` for the first wizard step. Add a row and two columns using the Bootstrap grid. In the first column, add a label and an `input` component to capture the transfer amount. Bind the `input` method to the `amount` attribute in the `transfer` model. In the second column, add a label and an `input` component to capture the transaction description. Bind the input to the `description` attribute in the `transfer` model. The implementation should look similar to this:

```
<div class="wizard-step" data-bind="if:
BankPortal.transferWizard.currentStep() == 2">
  <div class="row row-centered">
    <div class="col-md-8 col-centered">
      <div class="form-group">
        <label class="pull-left"
        for="transferAmount">Amount</label>
        <input id="transferAmount" class="form-control"
        data-bind="value: BankPortal.transfer.amount"/>
      </div>
    </div>

    <div class="col-md-8 col-centered">
      <div class="form-group">
        <label class="pull-left"
        for="transferDescription">Description</label>
        <input id="transferDescription" class="form-control"
        data-bind="value: BankPortal.transfer.description"/>
      </div>
    </div>
  </div>
</div>
```

The last wizard step should display the summary of inputs captured in step one and two. Locate the `div` with the third wizard. This `div` should be directly below the `div` for the second wizard step. Add a row and four columns. In each of the columns, use the data binding to display account from, account to, amount, and the description. For amount, use the currency custom binding we created in the previous chapter. The account attributes in the transfer model are observables; you will need to get the relevant information out of the observables and construct a string. Our implementation looks similar to this:

```
<div class="wizard-step" data-bind="if:
BankPortal.transferWizard.currentStep() == 3">
  <div class="row row-centered">
    <div class="col-md-8 col-centered">
```

```
        <strong>From account: </strong><span data-bind="text:
        BankPortal.transfer.fromAccount().summary.type + ' ' +
        BankPortal.transfer.fromAccount().summary.number"> </span>
    </div>
    <div class="col-md-8 col-centered">
        <strong>To account: </strong><span data-bind="text:
        BankPortal.transfer.toAccount().summary.type + ' ' +
        BankPortal.transfer.toAccount().summary.number"> </span>
    </div>
    <div class="col-md-8 col-centered">
        <strong>Amount: </strong><span data-bind="currency:
        BankPortal.transfer.amount"> </span>
    </div>
    <div class="col-md-8 col-centered">
        <strong>Description: </strong><span data-bind="text:
        BankPortal.transfer.description"> </span>
    </div>
  </div>
</div>
```

Run the application in the browser. Navigate to the transfers tab. You should now be able to see the input fields to capture the user input in the wizard steps. Try selecting the account to and account from. Move to the second step in the wizard and enter the amount to transfer and the transaction description. Move to the last step of the wizard. You should see the summary of the inputs captured in steps one and two. Try navigating back and forth in the wizard and change some inputs values. You should see the updated value in the summary. In our browser, it looks similar to this:

The next step is to modify the wizard module, in `wizard.js`, to notify the bank portal module that the user has clicked on **Done**. We will do this by adding a call back to the wizard module. This call back is a function of the bank portal module that gets executed by the wizard module when the user clicks on the **Done** button. Open the wizard module and add a variable to hold the call back:

```
/* call back on wizard done */
var doneCallBack;
```

Add a method to set the call back. Expose this method form the wizard module by adding it to the return statement of the module:

```
/* method sets the call back */
var setCallBack = function (callBack) {
doneCallBack = callBack;
};
```

Execute `doneCallBack` from the `done` method of the wizard module:

```
/* method for wizard done */
var done = function () {
  //Done reset wizard and call transfer
  console.log("User clicked done.....");
  currentStep(1);
  doneCallBack();
};
```

Open the bank portal module in `bankportal.js`. Add a method called `transferFunds`, which will submit a request to the server to transfer the funds:

```
/* method to submit transfer funds request to the server */
var transferFunds = function () {
  console.log("transfer funds ...");
};
```

We will get back to this method shortly to add the desired functionality. In the `init` method of the bank portal module, set the `transferFunds` method as the call back. The `init` method should now look similar to this:

```
var init = function () {
  /* add code to initialize this module */
  retrieveData();
  //model validation errors
  validationErrors = ko.validation.group(member, { deep: true });
```

```
    //set the call back for when the wizard is done
    transferWizard.setCallBack(transferFunds);
    //apply ko bindings
    ko.applyBindings(BankPortal);
};
```

In the body of the `transferFunds` method, make a call to the `transferFunds` method of the server and pass an unwrapped `transfer` observable. You can use `ko.toJS` to unwrap the `transfer` observable. The next step is to get the updated accounts from the server and refresh the accounts in the member model. Make a call to the `getAccounts` method of the server to retrieve the updated accounts information. Empty the `accounts` observable array in the `member` model and initialize it with the updated accounts. Lastly, clear the `transfer` model. Our implementation looks similar to this:

```
/* method to submit transfer funds request to the server */
var transferFunds = function () {
    console.log("Transferring amount " + transfer.amount() + " from
    account " + transfer.fromAccount().summary.number + " to account
    " + transfer.toAccount().summary.number);

    //submit the transfer request
    server.transferFunds(ko.toJS(transfer));

    //retrieve updated accounts
    var accounts = server.getAccounts();

    //remove all stale accounts
    member.accounts.removeAll();

    //add updated accounts to the model
    accounts.forEach(function(account) {
        member.accounts.push({summary: account.summary, transactions:
        ko.observableArray(account.transactions)});
    });

    //clear the transfer model
    clearTransferModel();
};
```

Notice the use of the `removeAll` method on the accounts observable array to remove all the accounts. The `clearTransferModel` method simply sets all the observables in the `transfer` model to null.

The last step is to notify the user that the funds have been transferred. To satisfy this requirement, we will display an alert component on the wizard. Add a flag in the wizard module to show or hide this alert component. We will call this flag showDoneMessage. Add this flag to the return statement of the module:

```
/* flag to show done message */
var showDoneMessage = ko.observable(false);
```

Add a doneMessage observable to hold the message to be displayed. As we want the wizard component to be generic, we will let the parent module define the message. In our case, the parent module is the bank portal. Modify the wizard module to take an addition parameter for the notification message. Initialize the observable for the message with the message passed to the wizard module:

```
/* Module for Wizard component */
var Wizard = function (steps, message) {
  /* add members here */
  ... ... ...
  /* message for when the wizard is done */
  var doneMessage = ko.observable(message);
  ... ... ...
  return {
    /* add members that will be exposed publicly */
    ... ... ...
    doneMessage: doneMessage,
    ... ... ...
  };
};
```

Set the showDoneMessage flag to true in the done method of the module. Set the flag to false in the method called next.

Open the view and add an alert construct in the div, containing the wizard component. Bind the text of the alert to the doneMessage observable of the wizard module. Use the visible binding to make it show or hide, based on the showDoneMessage flag. Our implementation looks similar to this:

```
<div class="panel panel-default">
  <div class="panel-heading">Transfer funds</div>
  <div class="panel-body">
    <div class="alert alert-success" role="alert"
    data-bind="visible:
    BankPortal.transferWizard.showDoneMessage">
      <strong>Done! </strong>
      <span data-bind="text:
      BankPortal.transferWizard.doneMessage"> </span>
    </div>
    ... ... ...
  </div>
</div>
```

The last step is to pass the message to be displayed to the wizard module from the bank portal module. To do this, modify the declaration of the wizard module and add the parameter for the notification message:

```
/* wizard module for transfer of funds */
var transferWizard = Wizard(3, "Funds transferred");
```

Open the application in the browser and navigate to the tabs for transfers. Select the accounts to transfer the funds between and move to the next step. Enter the amount you wish to transfer and the transaction description and move to the last step. The last step should show you the summary of the information from steps one and two. Click on the **Done** button if you are happy with your inputs. You should see an alert message notifying you that the funds have been transferred and the input fields should get cleared. Now navigate to the **Accounts** tab and view the balance of the accounts you transferred the funds between. The balance for the accounts should have been updated. View the transactions for the accounts. You should see a transaction with a category of debit for the account you selected to transfer funds from. Similarly, you should see a transaction with a category of credit for the account you selected to transfer funds to. Note that the fields in the wizard currently do not have any validation. Adding invalid user inputs will cause the application to fail. Try adding validation to fields in the wizard as an exercise. In our browser, the wizard looks similar to this:

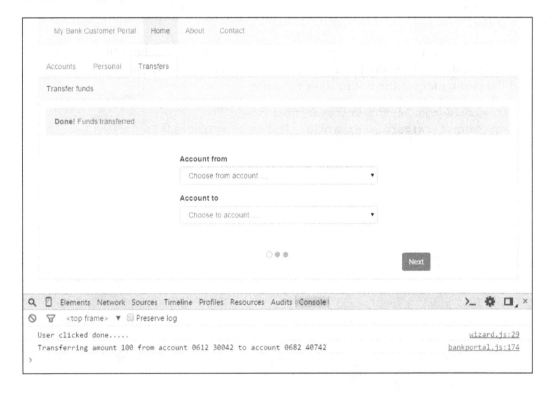

We have reached our final checkpoint for this chapter. The code for this checkpoint can be found at `chapter6\checkpoint6`.

Summary

In this chapter, we walked through enhancing the customer banking portal for MyBank with additional features that we started building in the previous chapter. In the first section, we implemented a user story to allow the users to update their personal information. We learned how to enable and disable the form fields and how to submit data to the server.

In the second section, we gave our users the ability to cancel the edited form and revert their changes. We discussed the different ways to achieve this and learned how to implement this requirement using the Knockout observables and the memento design pattern. In the third section, we implemented this user story about validating that the inputs for personal information in the form fields are valid.

In the last section, we implemented the user story of transferring funds between two accounts. We tackled this user story by dividing it into three aspects. The first aspect was to create the tab component for the transfer feature. This reinforced our understanding of how to use Knockout with a tab container. In the second aspect, we created a generic and reusable wizard component. In the third and the final aspect, we added the business feature of transferring funds between accounts using the wizard component we created. We learned how to use call backs to communicate events between modules and reinforced our learning of submitted requests to the server.

In the next chapter, we will enhance the customer banking portal further by securing it with a login screen and authentication token.

7
Securing the Customer Banking Portal

The customer banking portal, developed so far in the last two chapters, has the features the stakeholders at MyBank were looking for. Before we can go live with the portal, the CIO of MyBank wants the users of the portal to be authenticated using their username and password as credentials. We will continue with our iterative approach and implement the following user stories:

- As a member, I want to be able to login to customer banking portal using my authentication credentials
- As a member, I want to be informed if validation errors occur
- As a member, I want to be informed if an authentication error occurs
- As a member, I want to know who the logged in user is
- As a member, I want to be able to log out of the customer banking portal

This chapter is the third in the series on building a customer banking portal. It picks up the development from where we left it in the previous chapter and adds new features listed here. In this chapter, we will secure the customer banking portal using a login screen. The login screen will prompt the user for authentication credentials.

In this chapter, we will learn:

- The basics of securing a single page web application with token-based authentication
- How to use JSON Web Token (JWT) with single page web application
- How to develop a login screen for the application
- How to validate the user credentials
- How to handle failed login attempts
- How to sign out of the application

As before, we will continue taking the iterative approach to build the application. Each user story or feature has a corresponding checkpoint folder in the accompanying code.

Authentication mechanisms

We developed the interaction with the server in the last two chapters. In this chapter, we will explore different mechanisms by which we can provide authentication to the end user and protect the RESTful API endpoints. We will also implement an authentication approach based on **JSON Web Token (JWT)** for our customer banking portal. The following is a brief introduction of top four authentication mechanisms:

- **Basic authentication**: As the name suggests, this is the simplest mechanisms for protecting a RESTful endpoint or any web resource for that matter. It sends Base64 encoded username and password in the HTTP header and does not enforce any confidentiality protection. The username and password must be sent with every request. You can find the specifications for this mechanism on the Internet Engineering Task Force's website at `http://tools.ietf.org/html/rfc1945#section-11`.

- **OAuth 1.0a**: This provides authentication without ever directly passing the username and password to the application that provides the RESTful API endpoint. Instead, it relies on access tokens that can be revoked at any time by the application. It is the most widely used, tested, and secure protocol. You can find the specifications for this mechanism on the Internet Engineering Task Force's website at `http://tools.ietf.org/html/rfc5849`.

- **OAuth 2.0**: This is a completely different mechanism from OAuth 1.0a and is not backward-compatible. It greatly reduces the complexity of its predecessor by removing signatures from the specification. The encryption must be handled by Transport Layer Security (TLS) to make this mechanism secure. You can find the specifications for this mechanism on the Internet Engineering Task Force's website at `https://tools.ietf.org/html/rfc6749`.

- **Custom**: These authentication mechanisms should be avoided unless an industry standard does not meet your specific requirements, and you have a deep understanding of security concepts such as digital certificates, TLS, and access controls.

The example provided in this chapter uses a custom implementation of passing the access tokens between the client and server. The tokens are based on the JWT standard. The example shows how the client in a single page web application can be developed to use any of the authentication mechanisms mentioned here. In an ideal scenario, for our customer banking portal, we will use OAuth 2.0 with JWT as the token standard.

Basics of the token-based authentication

Before we get started with developing the user stories, it is important that we cover the basics of the token-based authentication—why it is a good fit for the RESTful API, and how it differs from traditional session cookies. In a single page application, such as our customer banking portal, the application is abstracted from the API that provides data. The authentication requirements thus shift from protecting the application to protecting the Restful API that provides the data. Using authentication tokens is one way of protecting Restful APIs.

Token versus session in cookies

Traditional websites use session cookies to secure web application. Once the user is logged in, the server places an HTTPOnly cookie in the response. The cookie contains an ID that identifies the user. It is passed to the server every time a request is made, allowing the server to identify the user.

 A cookie can be flagged as HttpOnly by the server to instruct the browser that the cookie must only be accessed by the server that placed it. A browser that implements HTTPOnly cookies properly should not be able to access them via JavaScript.

Session cookies have three main drawbacks:

- They are highly susceptible to **Cross-Site Request Forgery (CSRF)**
- They do not provide information about the logged in user to the single page application
- The state is kept on the server that hinders the server-side scalability

Using tokens is another way to authenticate the user without the drawbacks of session cookies described here. The general flow is that the web application sends a login request based on an authentication scheme. The authentication scheme is usually username and password-based. The server authenticates the request and returns a token. The token contains all the information required to identify the user and is usually signed to prevent any modifications to it and is sent over **Secure Sockets Layer (SSL)** to prevent **man-in-the middle attack**. It must be stored on the browser and sent to the server with every request.

> The **Open Web Application Security Project (OWASP)** is a good source of information if you want to learn more about web application vulnerabilities such as CSRF and man in the middle attack. Their article on CSRF can be found at `https://www.owasp.org/index.php/CSRF`.

Modern browsers have a few different ways of storing information locally. You can store the token in a JavaScript variable. The downside is that the token will be lost on page refresh. However, it can be stored in a client-side cookie. This approach has the overhead of cookie management. A better approach is to use the session storage of the browser. The session storage stores data only for the current session and is cleared when the user closes the browser window.

Storing the token in the browser using either of the approaches described here would still leave the application susceptible to **Cross-site Scripting (XSS)**. Good coding standards can ensure that your application is less vulnerable to XSS.

> Follow the prevention cheat sheet by OWASP to protect your application against XSS. The cheat sheet can be found at `https://www.owasp.org/index.php/XSS_(Cross_Site_Scripting)_Prevention_Cheat_Sheet`.

JSON Web Token

JSON Web Token (JWT) is a standard for authentication tokens based on JSON. The standard gives a structure to define the user. The token can be encrypted and signed for verification. As JWTs are verifiable and contain all the information required to identify the user, you do not need to hold the state of the logged in user on the server. You can read more about the standard at `https://tools.ietf.org/html/draft-ietf-oauth-json-web-token-32`.

JWT consists of three parts—header, payload, and signature. The token is transmitted as base 64 encoded string for each part separated by a dot (.). A token transmitted over the wire can look similar to this:

```
eyJ0eXAiOiJKV1QiLCJhbGciOiJIUzI1NiJ9.eyJpc3MiOiJteWJhbmsiLCJleHAiO
jE0MzQ4NzA0OTEyNTksInN1YiI6ImF1dGhlbnRpY2F0aW9uIHRva2VuIiwiZmlyc3
ROYW1lIjoiSm9obiIsImxhc3ROYW1lIjoiQ2l0aXplbiIsInVzZXJOYW1lIjoiam9
obi5jaXRpemVuIn0.U8c0TV8A_nj9JHZuoe5cHsjZo5MSK-5qTsM5Cbk1-wk
```

The header is a JSON string that states the token type and the algorithm used for hashing, for example:

```
{
    typ: "JWT",
    alg: "HS256"
}
```

The payload contains the claims that identifies the user. Some claims are reserved such as `iss`, `exp`, and `sub`. The `iss` claim identifies the issuer of the token, `exp` is the expiration, and `sub` is the subject. The following is an example of the payload:

```
{
    iss: "mybank",
    exp: 1654684812165,
    sub: "authentication token",
    firstName: "John",
    lastName: "Citizen",
    userName: "john.citizen"
}
```

The last part of the token is a hash of the header, payload, and a secret. The secret is a signature held by the server for verifying the token.

Now that we have learned some of the basics of token based authentication, it's time to start developing the authentication for our customer banking portal. We will be using JWTs for storing them in the browser's session storage.

Logging in to the application

The first user story of this chapter is about securing the application using a login screen and token-based authentication using JWT. We will implement the following flow:

1. The user accesses the customer banking portal via the browser.
2. The portal application looks for the authentication token to check whether the user is already authenticated or not.
3. The portal application displays the login screen to prompt the user for their username and password.
4. The user enters his/her username and password.
5. The portal application submits the username and password to the server.
6. The server validates the username and password and returns a token.
7. The portal application stores the token returned by the server.
8. The portal application makes a request to retrieve member data and passes the authentication token with the request.
9. The server validates the incoming authentication token and returns the requested member data.

You should start on this story by checking out code from `chapter6\checkpoint6`. This story requires an updated server stub. Download the `serverstub.js` and `jwt.js` files from `chapter7\server` and copy them to the `javascript` folder of your project overriding the existing `serverstub.js` file. Open the `bankportal.html` file and include `jwt.js` in the HTML header before `serverstub.js`. Run the application by opening the `bankportal.html` file in the browser. You will see that the application does not work anymore. This is because the new server stub expects an authentication token with the request to retrieve member data. We are now ready to develop this user story.

To implement and test this user story, we will:

*   Create a new module to handle authentication. This module will be responsible for holding the model to bind with the login form. The module will also make the authentication call to the server and store the authentication token.
*   Update the view to add a login screen and render the application based on whether the user is authenticated or not.
*   Refactor the portal module to use the authentication module.
*   Test the module using different user accounts.

Creating the authentication module

The first step is to create a module that will be responsible for handling the authentication with the server and storing the authentication token. We will call this module `Authenticator`. Create the `authenticator.js` file in the `javascript` folder and add a module skeleton to it. The module should accept the `server` module on creation. It should look similar to this:

```
/* Module for authenitcation  */
var Authenticator = function (serverModule) {
  /* add members here */

  /* the server module */
  var server = serverModule;

  return {
    /* add members that will be exposed publicly */
  };
};
```

Add a model to this module to hold the username and password. The fields must be Knockout observables so that we can bind them to the login form. Call the `credentials` model and add it to the `return` statement of the module. The model should look similar to this:

```
/* model for user credentials */
var credentials = {
  userName: ko.observable(),
  password: ko.observable()
};
```

The next step is to add a method to the module that calls the server method for authentication. The method exposed by the server is called `login` and takes username and password as parameters. On successful authentication, the `login` method of the server returns a JWT. The login method returns a `false` on an unsuccessful login attempt.

Add an observable to the `authenticator` module to store the authentication result and call it `authenticationToken`. Then, add a method to the `authenticator` module to call the `login` method of the server and store the result in the `authenticationToken` observable and also in the session storage of the browser. On successful login, we would like to inform the portal module about it so that it could continue with the application logic. We do this by adding a callback method to the `authenticator` module. Add a variable to store the portal module callback method. Also, add a method to set the callback and expose it in the `return` statement of the module.

Add a method to initialize this module; this method must get executed on module creation. Check for the authentication token in the session storage of the browser. It should initialize the `authenticationToken` observable with the token from session storage, otherwise, it should set it to false.

The last step is to add a method to the `authenticator` module that returns a `true` if the user has been authenticated, otherwise, `false`. Add this method as a pure computed observable that checks for the `authenticationToken` observable. Call the pure computed observable, `isAuthenticated`, and add it to the `return` statement of the `authenticator` module. After following the steps described here, the `authenticator` module should look similar to this:

```
/* Module for authenitcation */
var Authenticator = function (serverModule) {
  /* the server module */
  var server = serverModule;

/* authentication for the currently logged in user */
  var authenticationToken = ko.observable();

/* call back on successful login */
  var loginCallBack;

/* model for user credentials */
  var credentials = {
    userName: ko.observable(),
    password: ko.observable()
  };

  /* return the authentication token */
  var getAuthenticationToken = function () {
    return authenticationToken();
  };

  /* return true if user is authenticated, false otherwise */
```

```
  var isAuthenticated = ko.pureComputed(function() {
    return authenticationToken() != false;
  });

  /* login to the server */
  var login = function() {
    var token = server.login(credentials.userName(),
    credentials.password());
    authenticationToken(token);
    console.log("login" + authenticationToken());
    loginCallBack();
  };

  /* method sets the call back */
  var setCallBack = function (callBack) {
    loginCallBack = callBack;
  };

/* initialize the module */
var init = function () {
  var token = sessionStorage.getItem("token");
  if(token == null)
    authenticationToken(false)
  else
    authenticationToken(token)
}();

  return {
    /* add members that will be exposed publicly */
    isAuthenticated: isAuthenticated,
    credentials: credentials,
    getAuthenticationToken: getAuthenticationToken,
    setCallBack: setCallBack,
    login: login
  };
};
```

Creating the login screen

The next step is to add a login screen to the view. The user must be prompted for a username and password if an authentication token does not exist and if it does, the user should be allowed to use the application features.

Let's start by including an `authenticator` module to our application. Open the view in `bankportal.html` and include the `authenticator.js` file in the HTML header before the `include` for `bankportal.js`. Download the `bankportal.css` file from `chapter7\css` and replace it with the file in the `css` folder of the application. The new `bankportal.css` file contains styles for the login form.

Locate the first `div` element in the view. It should have `class="container"`. Add an `if` binding to this `div` element and bind it to the `isAuthenticated` method of the `authenticator` module. This `div` contains the main application and adding the `if` binding will make it not to appear if the user has not yet been authenticated.

Add a new `div` before the `div` element for main application that we modified earlier. We will call this new `div`, the login `div`. Add an `ifnot` binding to it and bind it to the `isAuthenticated` method of the `authenticator` module. This `div` will contain our login form and will only appear if the user is not authenticated. So far, it should look like this:

```
<div class="container" data-bind="ifnot:
BankPortal.authenticator.isAuthenticated">
  <!-- add login form here -->
</div>
<div class="container" data-bind="if:
BankPortal.authenticator.isAuthenticated">
... ... ...
</div>
```

The next step is to add a login form. The login form must have two input elements— one for capturing the username and the other for capturing the password. The form must also have a `submit` button. Add the form to the login `div`. Bind the username and the password input elements to the `credentials` model of the `authenticator` module. Bind the `submit` action of the form to the `login` method of the `authenticator` module. Use the `form-login` style class on the form element to give it the appropriate styling. Our implementation looks similar to this:

```
<div class="container" data-bind="ifnot:
BankPortal.authenticator.isAuthenticated">
  <form class="form-login" data-bind="submit:
  BankPortal.authenticator.login">
    <h2 class="form-login-heading">Please sign in</h2>
    <label for="inputUserName" class="sr-only">User name</label>
```

```
<input type="text" id="inputEmail" class="form-control"
    placeholder="User name" data-bind="value:
    BankPortal.authenticator.credentials.userName">
<label for="inputPassword" class="sr-only">Password</label>
<input type="password" id="inputPassword" class="form-control"
    placeholder="Password" data-bind="value:
    BankPortal.authenticator.credentials.password">
<button class="btn btn-lg btn-primary btn-block"
type="submit">Sign in</button>
    </form>
</div>
```

Note that the `authenticator` module is exposed through the `BankPortal` module.

Refactoring the BankPortal module

Now that we have created the `authenticator` module and updated the view with the login form, we can work on the last step of this user story. In this step, we will refactor the `BankPortal` module to use the `authenticator` module. Open the `BankPortal` module in `bankportal.js`. Add the `authenticator` module after the declaration of the sever module. Pass the server module as a parameter to the `authenticator` module and add the `authenticator` to the `return` statement of the `BankPortal` module:

```
/* Module for Customer banking portal application */
var BankPortal = function () {
  /* add members here */
  /* module to retrieve data from the server */
  var server = ServerStub();
  /* module for authentication */
  var authenticator = Authenticator(server);
  ... ... ...
    return {
    /* add members that will be exposed publicly */
    ... ... ...
    authenticator: authenticator
  };
}();
```

Next, we will create a method that will be called on successful authentication. We will set this method as the callback on the `authenticator` module. Create a method called `postAuthenticationInit`. In this method, check whether the user has been authenticated, and retrieve the data from the server by calling the `retrieveData` method. Also, create the validation errors in this method. Refactor the original `init` method of the `Bankportal` module to set the `postAuthenticationInit` method as the callback for the `authenticator` module and remove the call to the `retrieveData` method and creation of the validation errors. The `init` method should also call the `postAuthenticationInit` method to initialize the module with data in case the user is already authenticated. After the refactor, it should look similar to this:

```
/* call back for when authentication is successful */
var postAuthenticationInit = function() {
  if(authenticator.isAuthenticated()) {
    retrieveData();
    //model validation errors
    validationErrors = ko.validation.group(member, { deep: true
    });
  }
};
var init = function () {
  /* add code to initialize this module */

  //set the call back for when the wizard is done
  transferWizard.setCallBack(transferFunds);
  //set the call back for successful login
  authenticator.setCallBack(postAuthenticationInit);

  //apply ko bindings
  ko.applyBindings(BankPortal);
//init with data if user already authenticated
postAuthenticationInit();
};
```

We need to pass the authentication token to the server on every call we make so that the server knows who the logged in user is. The new server stub methods take the token as an additional parameter. Modify all the calls made to the server and add the token as a parameter. There should be four such calls. The following are the update server calls:

```
... ... ...
var data =
server.getMemberData(authenticator.getAuthenticationToken());
... ... ...
```

```
server.updatePersonalInformation(ko.toJS(member.personal),
authenticator.getAuthenticationToken());

... ... ...
server.transferFunds(ko.toJS(transfer),
authenticator.getAuthenticationToken());
... ... ...
var accounts = server.getAccounts(authenticator.
getAuthenticationToken());
... ... ...
```

Testing the application using different user accounts

Now that we have made all the changes required to implement this user story, we are ready to test the application. The two user accounts that are already setup on the server are john.citizen with a password, john123, and mark.person with a password, mark123.

 The session storage used for storing the authentication token will not work in Internet Explorer if the application is run from the local filesystem. Deploy the application on a web server and access it over HTTP for it to work with Internet Explorer. Alternatively, use a different browser.

Open the application in the browser. You should be presented with a login screen. Try logging in using the first account by entering john.citizen as the username and john123 as the password. The application should let you in as the user John, and displays John's accounts. Since the logout feature is not yet implemented, open the application in another browser window to login as a different user. Try logging in using the credentials for Mark. Try logging in using wrong credential and see what happens.

In our browser, this feature looks similar to the following screenshot:

For production systems, always use **Transport Layer Security** (TLS) with a strong certificate to prevent user data and authentication from being compromised.

We have reached our first checkpoint for this chapter. The code for this checkpoint can be found at `chapter7\checkpoint1`.

Validating the login form

This user story is about validating the login form for blank user inputs for username or password. This is similar to, and will re-enforce the concepts of form validation described in the previous chapters. To implement validation to the login form, we will:

- Add validation extenders to the credentials model
- Create errors group for the credentials model
- Modify the login form submit method to check for errors
- Update the view to add validation to the login form

Let's get started by opening the authenticator module and adding validation extenders to the credentials model:

```
/* model for user credentials */
var credentials = {
  userName: ko.observable().extend({ required: true}),
  password: ko.observable().extend({ required: true})
};
```

Now create the errors group for the credential model by adding the following line of code to the `init` method of the authenticator module:

```
/* initialize errors */
credentials.errors = ko.validation.group(credentials);
```

Next, we modify the `login` method of the `authenticator` module to check for errors. We show the errors if they exist and do not proceed with the login request to the server. After making this modification, the `login` method should look similar to this:

```
/* login to the server */
var login = function() {
  //check if validation errors occurred
```

```
    if (credentials.errors().length > 0) {
      console.log("Credentials model is invalid.....");
      credentials.errors.showAllMessages();
      return;
    }
    ... ... ...
  };
```

Lastly, we will update the view to add the validation to the login form. Open the view in `bankportal.html` and add a `div` element each, around the label, and input elements for username and password. Add the `validationElement` data binding to the `div` elements. Add a `validationOption` data binding to the `div` elements and configure it to not show the error messages. We do this as we do not want to show error messages; we only show error styles for the login form. After making the updates described here, the login form should look similar to this:

```
<form class="form-login" data-bind="submit:
BankPortal.authenticator.login">
  <h2 class="form-login-heading">Please sign in</h2>
  <div data-bind="validationOptions: {insertMessages: false},
  validationElement:
  BankPortal.authenticator.credentials.userName">
    <label for="inputUserName" class="sr-only">User name</label>
    <input type="text" id="inputEmail" class="form-control"
    placeholder="User name" data-bind="value:
    BankPortal.authenticator.credentials.userName">
  </div>
  <div data-bind="validationOptions: {insertMessages: false},
  validationElement:
  BankPortal.authenticator.credentials.password">
    <label for="inputPassword" class="sr-only">Password</label>
    <input type="password" id="inputPassword" class="form-control"
    placeholder="Password" data-bind="value:
    BankPortal.authenticator.credentials.password">
  </div>
  <button class="btn btn-lg btn-primary btn-block"
  type="submit">Sign in</button>
</form>
```

Open the application in the browser. Try hitting the **Sign in** button without entering anything for the username and password. You should now see the username and password fields highlighted with the error style. It should look similar to the following screenshot:

We have reached our second checkpoint for this chapter. The code for this checkpoint can be found at chapter7\checkpoint2.

Handling the authentication error

This user story is about displaying a message to the user if the login fails based on the username and password that the user has provided. To implement this user story, we will take the following steps:

- Add a flag to the authenticator module to show or hide the authentication error

- Modify the login method of the authenticator module to check for the authentication error

- Update the view to add an alert box with the authentication error

Let's get started by opening the authenticator module and adding an observable that will serve as a flag to show or hide the authentication error alert box:

```
/* flag to show authentication failed message */
var showAuthenticationFailed = ko.observable(false);
```

Add the preceding flag to the `return` statement of the authenticator module. Now modify the `login` method to check whether the server returns a `false` for the login call. In case of authentication failure, set the `showAuthenticationFailed` flag to `false` and do not proceed any further by returning out of the module. The `login` method of the `authenticator` module should look similar to this:

```
/* login to the server */
var login = function() {
    ... ... ...
    var token = server.login(credentials.userName(),
    credentials.password());
    if(token == false) {
        showAuthenticationFailed(true);
        return;
    }
    ... ... ...
};
```

Lastly, update the view to add an alert box with the authentication error. To do this, add the following code below the `Submit` button of the login form:

```
<div class="alert alert-danger" role="alert" data-bind="visible:
BankPortal.authenticator.showAuthenticationFailed">
<strong>Login failed!</strong> Invalid user name or
password</div>
```

The preceding code uses the visible binding to display the authentication alert box based on the `showAuthenticationFailed` flag.

Open the application in the browser and try adding an invalid username and password and hit the **Sign in** button. You should now see the authentication error alert box appear:

We have reached our third checkpoint for this chapter. The code for this checkpoint can be found at `chapter7\checkpoint3`.

Displaying the logged in user

In this user story, we will display the username of the logged in user on the screen. To implement this user story, we will take the following steps:

- Add a method to the authenticator module to extract and return the username from the JWT

- Update the view to display the logged in user in the navigation bar

Let's start by adding a method to the authenticator module. We will name this method `loggedInUser` and make it a pure observable so that it can be used in the view. We will extract the username form the JWT we received from the server. Recall the JWT structure described earlier in this chapter. The JWT is base64 encoded with dot (.) as the separator between head, body, and signature. To retrieve the username, we will split the token and then base64 decode the body. The body of the token contains the `userName` attribute, which the method should return. Our implementation of the pure computed observable looks similar to this:

```
/* return the user name of the logged in user */
var loggedInUser = ko.pureComputed(function () {
  var token = authenticationToken();
  var split = token.split("\.");
  var userPayload = JSON.parse(jwt.base64urldecode(split[1]));
  return userPayload.userName;
});
```

Add `loggedInUser` to the `return` statement of the authenticator module. Now we can update the view to display the username using the `loggedInUser` observable. Open the view in `bankportal.html` and locate the navigation bar. The navigation bar has the `nav` element. Within the navigation bar, locate the `div` with `id="navbar"`. Add another `ul` element to the `div` with an `li` element to display the username. You can use the `span` element to bind the text with the `loggedInUser` observable. Our implementation looks similar to this:

```
<nav class="navbar navbar-default">
  <div class="container-fluid">
    ... ... ...
    <div id="navbar" class="navbar-collapse collapse">
      <ul class="nav navbar-nav">
      ... ... ...
      </ul>
      <ul class="nav navbar-nav navbar-right">
        <li>
          <span class="navbar-text" data-bind="text:
          BankPortal.authenticator.loggedInUser" ></span>
```

```
        </li>
      </ul>
    </div>
  </div>
</nav>
```

Notice that I am using the `navbar-right` style class to pull the username to the right of the navigation bar.

Open the application in the browser. Login with `john.citizen` as the user. You should now see the username appear on the right-hand side of the navigation bar. It should look similar to this:

We have reached our fourth checkpoint for this chapter. The code for this checkpoint can be found at `chapter7\checkpoint4`.

Logging out of the application

In this user story, we will give the users the ability to be able to log out of the application. To implement the logout feature, we will:

- Add a method to the `authenticator` module to send a logout request to the server and reload the application

- Update the view to display the logout link

Let's start by adding a method to the authenticator module. We will name this method logout. This method should send a logout request to the server, clear the token stored in the session, and reload the application. The server invalidates the token on the logout request. Reloading the application will clear it from any data stored about the user. Add this method to the return statement of the authenticator module. Our implementation looks similar to this:

```
/* logout out of the application */
var logout = function() {
  server.logout(authenticationToken());
  sessionStorage.clear();
  document.location.reload(true);
};
```

Now we can update the view and add the logout link. We will modify the username in the navigation bar we developed in the previous user story to a dropdown and add the logout as an item. Make the modifications and bind the click of logout to the logout method in the authenticator module. The updated view should look similar to this:

```
<ul class="nav navbar-nav navbar-right">
  <li class="dropdown">
    <a href="#" class="dropdown-toggle" data-toggle="dropdown"
    role="button" aria-haspopup="true" aria-expanded="false"><span
    data-bind="text:
    BankPortal.authenticator.loggedInUser"></span>
    <span class="caret"></span></a>
    <ul class="dropdown-menu">
      <li><a href="#" data-bind="click:
      BankPortal.authenticator.logout">Logout</a></li>
    </ul>
  </li>
</ul>
```

Open the application in the browser. Login with `john.citizen` as the user. You should now see the username appear on the right-hand side of the navigation bar with a down arrow. Click on the username to see the **Logout** link. Try logging out as `john.citizen` and login as `mark.person`. It should look similar to this:

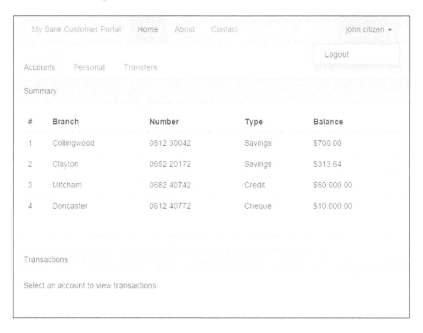

We have reached our final checkpoint for this chapter. The code for this checkpoint can be found at `chapter7\checkpoint5`.

Summary

In this chapter, we secured the customer banking portal based on username and password authentication scheme and token-based authentication. The first section of the chapter covered the commonly used authentication mechanisms, basics of token-based authentication, and saw how it differs from the traditional session cookie-based approach.

In the second section, we developed the login screen and applied the token-based authentication using JWT. This second covered the user input validation.

In the third section, we implemented error handling for a failed login attempt. The fourth section was about retrieving the logged in user from the authentication token and displaying the username on the screen. In the last section, we implemented the logout feature.

This was the last chapter in the series of developing the customer banking portal. In the next chapter, we will look at developing an editable grid with CRUD operations.

8

Building an Editable Products Grid with CRUD Operations

In this chapter we will walk through building an editable products grid application. This application will allow the users to create, view, update, and delete products. In the previous chapters, we used a server stub to mimic the server. However, in this chapter, we will learn how to develop a client to communicate with a real server, which exposes the RESTful services for CRUD operations. The products grid application will build and enhance the concepts learned in the previous chapters.

We will implement the following application features in this chapter:

- View a list of all the products, including product ID, name, description, and price
- Delete a product from the product list
- Add a new product to the product list
- Update an existing product

In this chapter, you will learn how to:

- Build a generic RESTful API client
- Perform create operation using HTTP POST
- Perform read operation using HTTP GET
- Perform update operation using HTTP PUT
- Perform delete operation using HTTP DELETE

- Work with observable arrays, `foreach` flow control and templating to render a table.

- Use `visible` binding to show or hide components

- Use `click` binding to capture button clicks and map them to CRUD operations

As we did in the previous chapters, we will be taking an iterative approach to building the products grid application. We will iteratively develop each feature listed here until the application evolves into a fully featured application. Each feature will have a corresponding checkpoint folder in the accompanying code. The folders are named `chapter8\checkpoint1`, `chapter8\checkpoint2`, and so on.

A word on REST

Representational State Transfer (**REST**) is an architecture style that exposes data and functionality using **Uniform Resource Identifiers** (**URIs**). It is independent of protocol or message format. Most web applications use RESTful web services over HTTP using JSON as the message format. The RESTful web services over HTTP use the following convention when mapping CRUD operations to HTTP methods:

CRUD operation	HTTP method
Create	POST
Read	GET
Update	PUT
Delete	DELETE

The RESTful web services are used in modern single page applications because they decouple the services from the user experience logic. They are also performant, lightweight, scalable, stateless, and maintainable.

The products grid application uses the RESTful web services to perform CRUD operations on the products. It exposes the following services:

Service description	HTTP method	URI	Message format
Add a product	POST	`http://[host:port]/products`	JSON
Retrieve all products	GET	`http://[host:port]/products`	JSON
Update a product	PUT	`http://[host:port]/products`	JSON
Delete a product	DELETE	`http://[host:port]/products/{id}`	JSON

The following is an example of message returned by HTTP GET
`http://[host:port]/products`:

```
[
    {
        "id":"#1000",
        "name":"Chess Periodicals",
        "description":"A book on chess periodicals",
        "price":100
    },
    {
        "id":"#2000",
        "name":"Strategy and Tactics",
        "description":"A book on chess strategy and tactics",
        "price":120
    }
]
```

Installing and running the sever

The first step before we start developing the user stories is to install and run the server. The server will expose the RESTful APIs for our products grid application. We will use Node.js as the server.

 Node.js is a server-side JavaScript-based platform for building network applications. You can learn about Node.js at `https://nodejs.org/`.

To install and run the server, perform the following steps:

1. Download and install `node.js` from `https://nodejs.org/`.
2. Create a folder for server module. Let's call it `ProductsServer`.

3. Navigate to the `ProductsServer` folder and install the `Restify` module using npm.

```
~
$ mkdir ProductsServer

~
$ cd ProductsServer/

~/ProductsServer
$ npm install restify

> dtrace-provider@0.6.0 install ProductsServer\node_modules\restify\node_modules\dtrace-provider
> node scripts/install.js

restify@4.0.3 node_modules\restify
├── assert-plus@0.1.5
├── escape-regexp-component@1.0.2
├── tunnel-agent@0.4.1
├── keep-alive-agent@0.0.1
├── negotiator@0.5.3
├── lru-cache@2.7.0
├── mime@1.3.4
├── formidable@1.0.17
├── node-uuid@1.4.3
├── qs@3.1.0
├── vasync@1.6.3
├── semver@4.3.6
├── spdy@1.32.4
├── once@1.3.2 (wrappy@1.0.1)
├── backoff@2.4.1 (precond@0.2.3)
├── verror@1.6.0 (extsprintf@1.2.0)
├── http-signature@0.11.0 (asn1@0.1.11, ctype@0.5.3)
├── dtrace-provider@0.6.0 (nan@2.0.9)
├── csv@0.4.6 (csv-generate@0.0.6, stream-transform@0.1.0, csv-stringify@0.0.8, csv-parse@1.0.0)
└── bunyan@1.5.1 (safe-json-stringify@1.0.3, mv@2.1.1)

~/ProductsServer
$_
```

4. Download `products-server.js` from `chapter8\server` to the `ProductsServer` folder.

5. Run the application using `node` and `products-server.js`.

```
~/ProductsServer
$ node products-server.js

restify listening at http://127.0.0.1:8080_
```

6. To test that the server is ready, open the browser and access `http://localhost:8080/products`. You should see the list of products in JSON format.

```
[{"id":"#1000","name":"Chess Periodicals","description":"A book on chess periodicals","price":100},
{"id":"#2000","name":"Strategy and Tactics","description":"A book on chess strategy and tactics","price":120},
{"id":"#3000","name":"Computer Chess","description":"Computer chess application","price":50},
{"id":"#4000","name":"Medieval Chess","description":"Medieval chess set","price":400},
{"id":"#5000","name":"End Games","description":"A book on end strategies","price":100},
{"id":"#6000","name":"Games of Individual Players","description":"A record of games by individual
players","price":200}]
```

Creating the skeleton

The next step is to create the skeleton before we can start building the application features. Follow these steps to create the skeleton; you should be familiar with these steps from earlier chapters.

First, create the folder structure for development:

1. Create the `ProductsGrid` folder. This is the main folder that houses our products grid application.

2. Add a `WebContent` folder under the `ProductsGrid` folder. This folder holds the content that gets published on the Web.

3. Add a `javascript` folder under the `WebContent` folder. As the folder name suggests, this folder will contain all our JavaScript files.

4. Add a `bootstrap` folder under the `WebContent` folder. This folder will contain the Bootstrap files.

Now that we have the folder structure in place, let's add the files to our folders by following these steps.

1. Add the Knockout library to the `javascript` folder.

2. Add the jQuery library to the `javascript` folder.

3. Add the Knockout validation plugin to the `javascript` folder.

4. Add Bootstrap to the `bootstrap` folder.

5. Create the `productsgrid.js` file under the `javascript` folder.

6. Download the `configureknockout.js` file from `chapter8\config` and copy it to the `javascript` folder.

7. Create the `productsgrid.html` file under the `WebContent` folder.

Following the preceding steps should result a folder structure that looks similar to this:

Now that we have created the folder structure, we can add code to our HTML and JavaScript files. Open the `productsgrid.html` file and add the following HTML code:

```
<!DOCTYPE HTML>
<html>
  <head>
    <meta http-equiv="Content-Type" content="text/html" />
    <title>Knockout : Products Grid</title>

    <link rel="stylesheet" href="bootstrap/css/bootstrap.min.css">

    <script type="text/javascript"
    src="javascript/jquery-2.1.3.min.js"></script>
    <script type="text/javascript"
    src="javascript/knockout-3.2.0.js"></script>
    <script type="text/javascript"
    src="javascript/knockout.validation.min.js"></script>
    <script type="text/javascript"
    src="javascript/configureknockout.js"></script>
```

```
    <script type="text/javascript"
    src="bootstrap/js/bootstrap.min.js"></script>
    <script type="text/javascript"
    src="javascript/productsgrid.js"></script>
  </head>
  <body>
    <div class="container">
      <div class="panel panel-default">
        <div class="panel-heading">Products</div>
        <div class="panel-body">
          <!-- Products grid -->
        </div>
      </div>
    </div>
  </body>
</html>
```

The preceding code references the required libraries and displays a panel header with the name of our application, Products. Open the productsgrid.js file and add the following code. The code defines our empty ProductsGrid module:

```
/* Module for products grid application */
var ProductsGrid = function () {
  /* add members here */

  var init = function () {
    /* add code to initialize this module */

        //apply ko bindings
        ko.applyBindings(ProductsGrid);
  };

  /* execute the init function when the DOM is ready */
  $(init);

  return {
    /* add members that will be exposed publicly */
  };
}();
```

View the application in the browser. It should give you a page with the panel header. We are now ready to start building our first feature.

Displaying the list of products

The first feature of this chapter is to display the list of products to the user. To implement this feature, we will:

- Create a new module that will serve as the client for our CRUD operations
- Update the products client module to add a method to retrieve products from the server
- Add the product model to the products grid module
- Update the products grid module to retrieve the list of products from the server
- Update the view to display the products

Let's get started by creating the client module for CRUD operations. Create a new JavaScript file called `productsclient.js` and add a blank module to it. The module should expect a base URL. This is the URL to the server. Add a method to the module to send a `GET` request to the server to retrieve the list of products. The method should expect a method that will be called on successful retrieval of data. Our implementation looks similar to this:

```
/* Module for products grid client */
var ProductsClient= function (url) {

    /* the base url for the rest service */
    var baseUrl = url;

    /* method to retrieve products */
    var getProducts = function(callback) {
      $.ajax({
          url: baseUrl + "/products",
          type: "GET",
          success: function(result) {
          console.log("Products retrieved: " +
          JSON.stringify(result));
            callback(result);
          }
      });
    };

    return {
      /* add members that will be exposed publicly */
      getProducts: getProducts
    };
};
```

Notice the use of the `$.ajax()` method. This method is provided by jQuery and is used to send AJAX requests to the RESTful web services. The `url` parameter in the object passed to the `$.ajax()` method specifies the URL of the service. The `type` parameter specifies the HTTP method, in this case, GET. The `success` parameter is a function that gets called on a successful response. We execute the callback method on a successful response.

Now we can add the model to the `ProductsGrid` module. The model should have observables for product ID, name, description, and price. To construct the model, we will create a method that takes a product returned by the server, constructs the model with the observables, and returns it. Our implementation looks similar to this:

```
/* model for products */
var productModel = function(item) {
  this.data = {};
  this.data.id = ko.observable(item.id);
  this.data.name = ko.observable(item.name);
  this.data.description = ko.observable(item.description);
  this.data.price = ko.observable(item.price);
};
```

Add an observable array to the `ProductsGrid` module that will hold the list of products. Add the observable array to the `return` statement of the module as we will access it from the view:

```
/* product observable array */
var products = ko.observableArray();
```

Next, we use the client module to retrieve and populate the `products` observable array. Add the `ProductsClient` module to the `ProductsGrid` module and pass the base URL of the server:

```
/* add members here */
var client = ProductsClient("http://localhost:8080");
```

Note that I am using localhost on port 8080. You should use the hostname and port appropriate to your environment. The hostname and port should ideally be externalized to a configuration file. Add two methods to the `ProductsGrid` module; one to retrieve the list of products using the client:

```
/* method to retrieve products using the client */
var retrieveProducts = function () {
  console.log("Retrieving products from server ...");
  client.getProducts(retrieveProductsCallback);
};
```

Add another method to act as the callback for when the data arrives back form the server. The call back method should construct products using the `productModel` method we created earlier and populate the `products` observable array. Here is our implementation of this method:

```
/* callback for when the products are retrieved from the server */
var retrieveProductsCallback = function (data) {
  data.forEach(function(item) {
    products.push(new productModel(item));
  });
};
```

The last step before we can move on to developing the view to call the `retrieveProducts` method from the ProductsGrid, init:

```
var init = function () {
  /* add code to initialize this module */
  retrieveProducts();

  //apply ko bindings
  ko.applyBindings(ProductsGrid);
};
```

We are now ready to work on the view. Open the view in the `productsgrid.html` file and locate the `div` element with `class="panel-body"`. Add an HTML `table` with columns for ID, name, description, and price. Use the `foreach` binding to bind the table body to the `products` observable array in the `ProductsGrid` module. Use the `text` binding for ID, name, and description. Use the `currency` binding for price. Our implementation looks similar to this:

```
<div class="panel-body">
  <table class="table">
    <thead>
      <tr>
        <th>ID</th>
        <th>Name</th>
        <th>Description</th>
        <th>Price</th>
      </tr>
    </thead>
    <tbody data-bind="foreach: ProductsGrid.products">
      <tr>
        <td data-bind="text: data.id"></td>
```

```
        <td data-bind="text: data.name"></td>
        <td data-bind="text: data.description"></td>
        <td data-bind="currency: data.price"></td>
      </tr>
    </tbody>
  </table>
</div>
```

Make sure that the server is running and open the application in browser. You should be able to see the products grid. In our browser, it looks similar to the following screenshot:

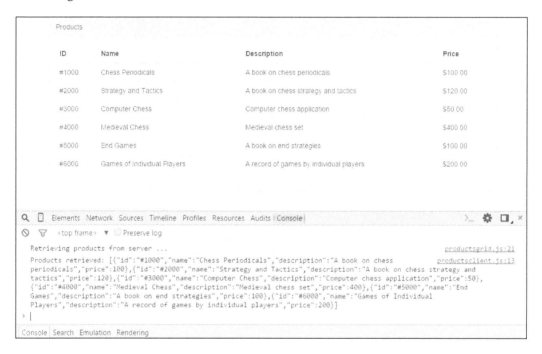

We have reached our first checkpoint for this chapter. The code for this checkpoint can be found at `chapter8\checkpoint1`.

Deleting a product

The second feature of this application is about deleting a product from the products grid. To implement this feature, we will:

- Update the products client module to add a method to send a request to the server to delete a product

- Update the products grid module to add a method to delete a product

- Update the view to add a new column to the grid that will contain a button for the delete action

Let's get started by updating the `ProductsClient` module. Open the `ProductsClient` module in the `productsclient.js` file and add a method to send an HTTP DELETE request to `http://[host:port]/products/{id}`. The method should expect the product model and a callback method as parameters. The callback method should get executed on successful response from the server. As used before to send the HTTP GET request, use the `$.ajax()` method provided by jQuery to send the HTTP DELETE request. Don't forget to add the method to the `return` statement of the `ProductsClient` module. Our implementation looks similar to this:

```
/* method to delete a product */
var deleteProduct = function(product, callback) {
  console.log("Deleting product with id [" + product.data.id() +
  "]");
  $.ajax({
    url: baseUrl + "/products/" + product.data.id(),
    type: "DELETE",
    success: function(result) {
      callback(product);
    }
  });
};
```

We can now update the `ProductsGrid` module to use the `deleteProduct` method from the `ProductsClient` module. Open the `ProductGrid` module and add a method to call the `deleteProduct` method of the `ProductsClient` module. This method should expect the product to be deleted and pass it to the `deleteProduct` method of the `ProductsClient` module along with a callback method. We will create the callback method in the next step. Add this newly created method to the `return` statement of the `ProductsGrid` module. This method should look similar to this:

```
/* method to send delete request to the client */
var deleteProduct = function (product) {
  client.deleteProduct(product, deleteProductCallback);
};
```

Now create a callback method, `deleteProductCallback`, which expects a product model as its parameter and removes it from the `products` observable array. Here is our implementation:

```
/* callback on successful delete request */
var deleteProductCallback = function (product) {
  products.remove(product);
  console.log("Product with id [" + product.data.id()+ "]
  deleted");
};
```

The final step is to update the view. Open the view in the `productsgrid.html` file and add a new column to the products table; call it actions. Add an anchor element to the column and bind it to the `deleteProduct` method to the `ProductsGrid` module. The table should now look similar to this:

```
<table class="table">
  <thead>
    <tr>
      <th>ID</th>
      <th>Name</th>
      <th>Description</th>
      <th>Price</th>
      <th>Actions</th>
    </tr>
  </thead>
  <tbody data-bind="foreach: ProductsGrid.products">
    <tr>
      <td data-bind="text: data.id"></td>
      <td data-bind="text: data.name"></td>
      <td data-bind="text: data.description"></td>
      <td data-bind="currency: data.price"></td>
      <td><a href data-bind="click:
      ProductsGrid.deleteProduct">Delete</a></td>
    </tr>
  </tbody>
</table>
```

Open the application in the browser. You should now see the actions column with a link to delete a product. Click on the **Delete** link to delete a product. In our browser, the application looks similar to the following screenshot:

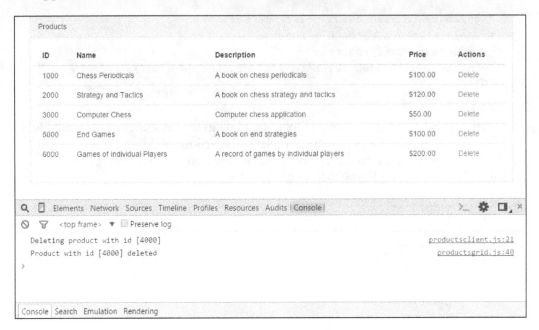

We have reached the second checkpoint for this chapter. The code for this checkpoint can be found at `chapter8\checkpoint2`.

Adding a product

The third feature of this application is about adding a product to the products grid. To implement this feature, we will:

- Update the products client module to add a method to send a request to the server to add a new product
- Update the product model to add a flag to switch the product between edit and display mode
- Update the products grid module to create a method to add a product
- Update the products grid module to create a method to save the product
- Update the view to create a link to add a product and capture user input

Let's get started by updating the `ProductsClient` module. Open the `ProductsClient` module in the `productsclient.js` file and add a method to send HTTP `POST` request to `http://[host:port]/products`. The method should expect the product model and a callback method as parameters. The callback method should get executed on successful response from the server. As used before to send the HTTP `DELETE` request, use the `$.ajax()` method provided by jQuery to send the HTTP `POST` request. Add a `data` parameter to the object passed to `$.ajax()` and assign it the product model as a JSON string. You can use `JSON.stringify()` method for this. Add another parameter, `contentType`, and assign the `application/json` value. This parameter tells the sever that the message is the request of type JSON. The server will create the product on the backend and return a generated ID of the product. Don't forget to add the method to the `return` statement of the `ProductsClient` module. Our implementation looks similar to this:

```
/* method to add a product */
var addProduct = function(product, callback) {
  var plainProduct = ko.toJS(product.data);
  console.log("Saving product [" + JSON.stringify(plainProduct) +
  "]");
  $.ajax({
    url: baseUrl + "/products",
    type: "POST",
    data:  JSON.stringify(plainProduct),
    contentType: "application/json",
    success: function(id) {
      callback(product, id);
    }
  });
};
```

Update the product model to add a flag that indicates the display mode of the product. The display mode can either be `edit` or `view`. We will use this flag in the view to render the input component that capture the user input for the new product. The updated product model should look similar to this:

```
/* model for products */
var productModel = function(item, itemMode) {
  this.data = {};
  this.data.id = ko.observable(item.id);
  this.data.name = ko.observable(item.name);
  this.data.description = ko.observable(item.description);
  this.data.price = ko.observable(item.price);
  this.diplayMode = ko.observable(itemMode);
};
```

Add an attribute to the module that represents the two display modes; add this attribute to the return statement of the module as we will need to access it from the view:

```
/* display modes for the grid */
var displayMode = {
  view: "VIEW",
  edit: "EDIT"
};
```

Modify the `retrieveProductsCallback` method to pass the display mode for the new products being added to the `products` observable array.

The next step is to update the `ProductsGrid` module to add a method to add a new blank product to the products grid. The display mode of this new product must be `edit` to allow the user to enter the product details. Here is our implementation:

```
/* method to add a blank product to the products array */
var addProduct = function () {
  var item = { sku: null, name: null, description: null, price:
  null};
  products.push(new productModel(item, displayMode.edit));
};
```

We can now update the `ProductsGrid` module to use the `addProduct` method from the `ProductsClient` module. Add a method to the `ProductsGrid` module that uses the `addProduct` method of the `ProductsClient` module:

```
/* method to send add request to the client */
var saveProduct = function (product) {
  client.addProduct(product, saveProductCallback);
};
```

Now, create a call back method, `saveProductCallback`, which expects a product model and the product ID returned by the server as its parameters. The method sets the product ID and the display mode to `view`. Here is our implementation:

```
/* callback on successful add request */
var saveProductCallback = function (product) {
product.data.id(id);
  product.diplayMode(displayMode.view);
  console.log("Product saved with id [" + product.data.id() +
  "]");
};
```

We are now ready to update the view. Open the view in the `productsgrid.html` file and add a link at the bottom of the products table to add a new product:

```
<a href data-bind="click: ProductsGrid.addProduct">+ Add a
Product</a>
```

Use the `click` binding and bind the link to the `addProduct` method of the `ProductsGrid` module. Next, add an `if` binding to the table `tr` element and make it render only if the display mode of the product is `view`. Add another `tr` element and use the `if` binding to make it render only if the display mode of the product is `edit`. In this new `tr` element, use input components and bind them to the product model. Lastly, add a save link in the actions column to save the newly created product. Use the `click` binding and bind it to the `saveProduct` method of the `ProductsGrid` module. The modified products table should look similar to this:

```
<table class="table">
  <thead>
    <tr>
      <th>ID</th>
      <th>Name</th>
      <th>Description</th>
      <th>Price</th>
      <th>Actions</th>
    </tr>
  </thead>
  <tbody data-bind="foreach: ProductsGrid.products">
    <tr data-bind="if: diplayMode() ===
    ProductsGrid.displayMode.view">
      <td data-bind="text: data.id"></td>
      <td data-bind="text: data.name"></td>
      <td data-bind="text: data.description"></td>
      <td data-bind="currency: data.price"></td>
      <td><a href data-bind="click:
      ProductsGrid.deleteProduct">Delete</a></td>
    </tr>
    <tr data-bind="if: diplayMode() ===
    ProductsGrid.displayMode.edit">
      <td data-bind="text: data.id">
      </td>
      <td>
        <input type="text" class="form-control"
        data-bind="value: data.name" />
      </td>
      <td>
```

```
        <input type="text" class="form-control" data-bind="value:
        data.description" />
    </td>
    <td>
        <input type="text" class="form-control" data-bind="value:
        data.price" />
    </td>
    <td>
        <a href data-bind="click:
        ProductsGrid.saveProduct">Save</a> |
        <a href data-bind="click:
        ProductsGrid.deleteProduct">Delete</a>
    </td>
  </tr>
 </tbody>
</table>
```

Open the application in the browser. You should now see a link at the bottom of the grids table to add a product. Click on the add product link to add a product. A new row should appear with input boxes to capture the user input. Enter the product details and click on **Save**. You should see the new product added to the products grid. In our browser, the application looks similar to this:

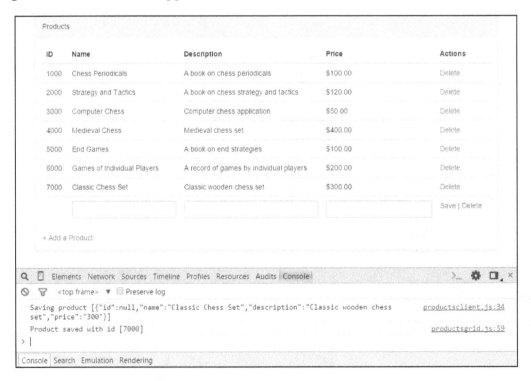

We have reached the third checkpoint for this chapter. The code for this checkpoint can be found at `chapter8\checkpoint3`.

Updating a product

The final feature of this chapter is about updating a product in the products grid. To implement this feature, we will:

- Update the products client module to add a method to send a request to the server to update a product
- Update the products grid module to create a method to edit a product
- Update the products grid module to create a method to update the product
- Update the view to create a link to update the product

Let's get started by updating the `ProductsClient` module. Open the `ProductsClient` module in the `productsclient.js` file and add a method to send HTTP PUT request to `http://[host:port]/products`. The method should expect the product model and a callback method as parameters. The callback method should get executed on successful response from the server. As used before to send the HTTP PUT request, use the `$.ajax()` method provided by jQuery to send the HTTP POST request. Add a `data` parameter to the object passed to `$.ajax()` and assign it the product model as a JSON string. You can use `JSON.stringify()` method from this. Add another parameter, `contentType`, and assign the value, `application/json`. This parameter tells the server that the message is a request is of type **JSON**. Don't forget to add the method to the `return` statement of the `ProductsClient` module. Our implementation looks similar to this:

```
/* method to update a product */
var updateProduct = function(product, callback) {
  var plainProduct = ko.toJS(product.data);
  console.log("Updating product [" + JSON.stringify(plainProduct)
  + "]");
  $.ajax({
    url: baseUrl + "/products",
    type: "PUT",
    data:  JSON.stringify(plainProduct),
    contentType: "application/json",
    success: function(result) {
      callback(product);
    }
  });
};
```

The next step is to update the `ProductsGrid` module to add a method to switch a product to the `edit` mode. The method simply calls the `displayMode` observable of the product model. Add this method to the `return` statement of the `ProductsGrid` module:

```
/* method to edit a product */
var editProduct = function (product) {
  product.displayMode(displayMode.edit);
};
```

We can now update the `ProductsGrid` module to use the `udpateProduct` method from the `ProductsClient` module. Add a method to the `ProductsGrid` module that uses the `updateProduct` method of the `ProductsClient` module:

```
/* method to send update request to the client */
var updateProduct = function (product) {
  client.updateProduct(product, updateProductCallback);
};
```

Now, create a callback method `updateProductCallback` which accepts a product model as its parameter. The method should change the display mode to `view`. Here is the implementation:

```
/* callback on successful update request */
var updateProductCallback = function (product) {
  console.log("Product updated with id [" + product.data.id() +
  "]");
  product.displayMode(displayMode.view);
};
```

We are now ready to update the view. Open the view in the `productsgrid.html` file and add a link to edit a product in the actions column of row for the `view` mode. Bind the click of the link to the `editProduct` method we created in the earlier step:

```
<tr data-bind="if: diplayMode() === ProductsGrid.displayMode.view
">
  <td data-bind="text: data.id"></td>
  <td data-bind="text: data.name"></td>
  <td data-bind="text: data.description"></td>
  <td data-bind="currency: data.price"></td>
  <td>
    <a href data-bind="click: ProductsGrid.editProduct">Edit</a>
    | <a href data-bind="click:
      ProductsGrid.deleteProduct">Delete</a>
  </td>
</tr>
```

In the products grid row for `edit` mode, add a link to update the product and bind it to the `updateProduct` method of the `ProductsGrid` module. Make the link only appear if the ID exists for the product; you can use the `visible` binding to achieve this. Similarly, make the save link to only appear if the product does not have an ID. Here is our implementation:

```
<tr data-bind="if: diplayMode() ===
ProductsGrid.displayMode.edit">
  <td data-bind="text: data.id">
  </td>
  <td>
    <input type="text" class="form-control" data-bind="value:
    data.name" />
  </td>
  <td>
    <input type="text" class="form-control" data-bind="value:
    data.description" />
  </td>
  <td>
    <input type="text" class="form-control" data-bind="value:
    data.price" />
  </td>
  <td>
    <a href data-bind="visible: data.id() != null, click:
    ProductsGrid.updateProduct">Update</a>
    <a href data-bind="visible: data.id() == null, click:
    ProductsGrid.saveProduct">Save</a> |
    <a href data-bind="click:
    ProductsGrid.deleteProduct">Delete</a>
  </td>
</tr>
```

Open the application in the browser. For each row of the products grid, you should now see a link to edit the product. Click on the **Edit** product link to edit the product. The product row should switch to `edit` mode. Update the update details and click on the **Update** link. You should see the product updated in the products grid and return back to display mode. In our browser, the application looks similar to this:

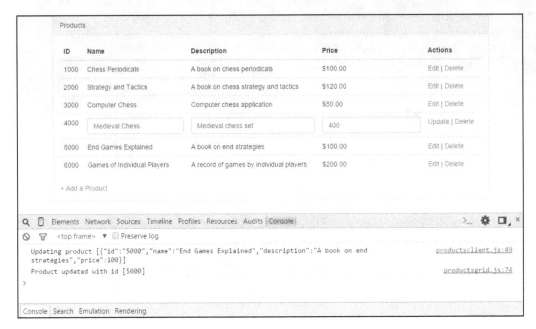

We have reached the final checkpoint for this chapter. The code for this checkpoint can be found at `chapter8\checkpoint4`.

Summary

In this chapter, we walked through building an editable products grid application. The application integrated with a server through the RESTful web services. The features of the application included displaying, deleting, adding, and updating products. The main focus of the chapter was learning how to perform CRUD operations using the RESTful web services.

We stared the chapter with a brief overview of the RESTful web services and the API calls the products grid server exposed. We then moved on to installing and running the server using Node.js before we started developing the application features.

The first feature of the products grid application was to retrieve the list of products from the server using an HTTP GET request and displaying the products in a grid. The second feature was about deleting a product. We used HTTP DELETE request to achieve this. The third feature was the ability to add a product. HTTP POST request was used to add a product. The last feature was the ability to update an existing product. HTTP PUT request was used to update a product on the server.

In the next, the final chapter of the book, we will look at using Google Maps API with Knockout.

Using Google Maps APIs with Knockout

9

In this chapter, we will walk through building an application that uses Google Maps APIs. The application will allow the users to enter address information using the `autocomplete` feature of the API and retrieve address details. The application will render a map and allow the users to place markers on it. The users will also be able to get directions between two addresses both as description and route on the map.

We will implement the following application features in this chapter:

- Capture from and to addresses using address `autocomplete`
- View detailed address information
- View a map
- Place markers on the map for addresses
- View route on the map between two markers

In this chapter, you will learn how to:

- Build a generic component with custom binding handler to capture address using the Google Maps APIs places library
- Retrieve and display detailed address information
- Build a generic component with custom binding handler to render a map
- Place markers on the map
- Use subscribers to interact with the map based on changes to the model
- Use the Google Maps APIs direction service to get directions from one address to the other
- Display route between two markers on a map

We will follow our pattern of iteratively developing each feature listed here until the application evolves into a fully featured application. Each feature will have a corresponding checkpoint folder in the accompanying code. The folders are named chapter9\checkpoint1, chapter9\checkpoint2, and so on.

Creating the skeleton

The first step is to create the skeleton before we can start building the application features. Follow these steps to create the skeleton. You should be familiar with these steps from earlier chapters.

Create the folder structure for development by following these steps:

1. Create the folder, MapsApplication. This is the main folder that houses our products grid application.
2. Add a WebContent folder under the MapsApplication folder. This folder holds content that gets published to the Web.
3. Add a javascript folder under the WebContent folder. As the folder name suggests, this folder will contain all our JavaScript files.
4. Add bootstrap folder under the WebContent folder. This folder will contain the Bootstrap files.

Now that we have the folder structure in place, let's add the files to our folders by following these steps.

1. Add the Knockout library to the javascript folder.
2. Add the jQuery library to the javascript folder.
3. Add Bootstrap to the bootstrap folder.
4. Create the mapsapplication.js file under the javascript folder.
5. Create the mapsapplication.html file under the WebContent folder.

Following these steps should result in a folder structure that looks similar to this:

Now that we have created the folder structure, we can add code to our HTML and JavaScript files. Open the `mapsapplication.html` file and add the following HTML code:

```html
<!DOCTYPE HTML>
<html>
  <head>
    <meta http-equiv="Content-Type" content="text/html" />
    <title>Knockout : Maps Application</title>

    <link rel="stylesheet" href="bootstrap/css/bootstrap.min.css">

    <script type="text/javascript"
    src="javascript/jquery-2.1.3.min.js"></script>
    <script type="text/javascript"
    src="javascript/knockout-3.2.0.js"></script>
    <script type="text/javascript"
    src="bootstrap/js/bootstrap.min.js"></script>
    <script type="text/javascript"
    src="javascript/mapsapplication.js"></script>
  </head>
  <body>
    <div class="container">
      <div class="row">
        <div class="col-md-12">
          <div class="panel panel-default">

            <div class="panel-heading">Address</div>
            <div class="panel-body">
            </div>
```

```
          </div>
        </div>
      </div>
    </div>
  </body>
</html>
```

The preceding code references the required libraries and displays a page with a panel with the heading, Address. Open the mapsapplication.js file and add the following code; the code defines our empty MapsApplication module:

```
/* Module for maps application */
var MapsApplication = function () {
  /* add members here */

  var init = function () {
    /* add code to initialize this module */
    ko.applyBindings(MapsApplication);
  };

  /* execute the init function when the DOM is ready */
  $(init);

  return {
    /* add members that will be exposed publicly */
  };
}();
```

View the application in the browser. It should give you a page with the panel header. We are now ready to start developing our first application feature.

Capturing address using autocomplete

The first feature of this chapter is about capturing address using the autocomplete feature of places library provided by the Google Maps APIs. To implement this feature, we will:

- Add reference to the Google Maps APIs library in the view
- Create the model to hold the address information
- Create custom binding handler for the address autocomplete input component
- Add the autocomplete input components to the view and bind them to use the custom binding handler

Let's get started by adding reference to the Google Maps APIs to the view. Open the view in the `mapsapplication.html` file and add the highlighted line of code in the HTML header:

```
<!DOCTYPE HTML>
<html>
  <head>
    <meta http-equiv="Content-Type" content="text/html" />
    <title>Knockout : Maps Application</title>

    <link rel="stylesheet" href="bootstrap/css/bootstrap.min.css">

    <script type="text/javascript"
    src="javascript/jquery-2.1.3.min.js"></script>
    <script type="text/javascript"
    src="javascript/knockout-3.2.0.js"></script>
    <script type="text/javascript"
    src="bootstrap/js/bootstrap.min.js"></script>
    <script
    src="https://maps.googleapis.com/maps/api/
    js?v=3.exp&signed_in=true&libraries=places"></script>

    <script type="text/javascript"
    src="javascript/mapsapplication.js"></script>
  </head>
    ... ... ...
</html>
```

The code pulls the required libraries from Google. Notice the `libraries=places` query parameter at the end of the URL. This query parameter instructs the Google Maps APIs that we require the `places` library, which we will use to retrieve the address details. The query parameter, `v=3.exp`, specifies that we require the experimental release of the Google Maps API version 3. The `signed_in=true` query parameter specifies that the map will be tailored to the signed in Google account user.

We are using the experimental release of Google JavaScript Maps API version 3 for developing maps application in this chapter. Use stable release versions of the API and obtain an API key to develop commercial applications.

Next, we will add a model to the `MapsApplication` module in the `mapsapplication.js` file to hold the addresses returned by the maps API. To do this, open the `MapsApplication` module and add the following code:

```
/* model to hold addresses */
var mapsModel = {
    fromAddress: ko.observable(),
    toAddress: ko.observable()
};
```

Note that we have two attributes in our model: one to capture address from and another to capture address to. Add the `mapsModel` attribute to the `return` statement of the module as we will access this attribute from the view.

The next step is to create a custom Knockout binding handler, which will apply `autocomplete` feature to an HTML `input` element. We will use the `Autocomplete` class provided by the Google Maps APIs for this. The following is the basic construct:

```
var autocomplete = new google.maps.places.Autocomplete(
element,{ types: ['geocode'] });
```

The first parameter to the `Autocomplete` class is the HTML element the feature will get applied to. The second parameter is `AutocompleteOptions`. You can find out about the options that can be set using the `AutocompleteOptions` class from the API reference on the Google Maps APIs website. The option we are using in our preceding example is `types`. This specifies the type of predictions to return. In our example, `types: ['geocode']` instructs the API to return only the geocoding results.

To create the custom binding handler for the `autocomplete` component, open the `MapsApplication` module in the `mapsapplication.js` file and create a method called `configureBindingHandlers`. Call this method from the `init` method of the module so that the custom binding handlers get created on module initialization. Add a custom binding called `addressAutoComplete`. This binding handler should apply the `Autocomplete` class to the HTML element passed in as the parameter. The binding handler should also add an event listener that retrieves the address and updates our model. Our implementation looks similar to this:

```
/* method to add custom binding handlers to knockout */
var configureBindingHandlers = function() {
  /* custom binding for address auto complete */
  ko.bindingHandlers.addressAutoComplete = {
    init: function(element, valueAccessor){
      // create the autocomplete object
      var autocomplete = new google.maps.places.Autocomplete(
      element,{ types: ['geocode'] });
```

```
        // when the user selects an address from the dropdown,
        populate the address in the model.
        var value = valueAccessor();
        google.maps.event.addListener(autocomplete, 'place_changed',
        function() {
          var place = autocomplete.getPlace();
          console.log(place);
          value(place);
        });
      }
    };
  };
```

We are now ready to work on the view. Open the view in the `mapsapplication.`
`html` file and locate the `div` element with `class="panel-body"`. Add two HTML
`input` components with labels—one to capture address from and another to capture
address to. Use the `addressAutoComplete` binding on the `input` components to
apply the autocomplete feature to the `input` components and store the result in our
model. It should look similar to this:

```
<div class="panel panel-default">
  <div class="panel-heading">Address</div>
  <div class="panel-body">
    <div id="addressFromFields" class="form-group">
      <label for="autocompleteFromAddress">From address</label>
      <input id="autocompleteFromAddress" class="form-control"
      data-bind="addressAutoComplete:
      MapsApplication.mapsModel.fromAddress" placeholder="Enter
      your from address" type="text"></input>
    </div>
    <div id="addressToFields" class="form-group">
      <label for="autocompleteToAddress">To address</label>
      <input id="autocompleteToAddress" class="form-control"
      data-bind="addressAutoComplete:
      MapsApplication.mapsModel.toAddress" placeholder="Enter your
      to address" type="text"></input>
    </div>
  </div>
</div>
```

Open the application in your browser and try typing an address in one of the address fields. You should see the `autocomplete` dropdown with predictions of valid addresses as you type. The address details object returned by the Google Maps APIs should get logged in the console on selection. In our browser, it looks similar to this:

We have reached our first checkpoint for this chapter. The code for this checkpoint can be found at `chapter9\checkpoint1`.

Displaying address details

The second feature is about retrieving and displaying the address details. To implement this feature, we will:

- Modify the model to capture address details
- Extract the address details from Google Maps APIs place object and populate the model
- Update the view to display the address details

Let's get started by modifying the model we created previously to capture address details. First, create a generic function to construct the address model. The address model should have attributes that you want to capture and display, such as street number and name. Here is our implementation:

```
/* generic model for address */
var AddressModel = function() {
  this.location = ko.observable();
  this.streetNumber = ko.observable();
  this.streetName = ko.observable();
  this.city = ko.observable();
  this.state = ko.observable();
  this.postCode = ko.observable();
  this.country = ko.observable();
};
```

Note the use of observables in `AddressModel`. This will allow you to do two-way binding between the view and model. The next step is to extract the address information from object of the `google.maps.places.PlaceResult` class returned by the `google.maps.places.Autocomplete getPlace()` method. Create a method called `populateAddress` that takes two parameters. The first parameter is the place object which is retrieved using `getPlace()` method and the second parameter is the value of `addressAutoComplete` binding. This method should extract the address information from place object and populate the model using the `AddressModel` observable. Consult the Google Maps APIs reference to get familiar with how the address information is structured in the `google.maps.places.PlaceResult` class.

 At the time of writing, the Google Maps APIs reference for experimental version 3 could be found at `https://developers.google.com/maps/documentation/javascript/3.exp/reference`.

The implementation of extracting the address information from the place object retrieved using the getPlace() method consists of an addressComponents object and a populateAddress method. The addressComponents object defines the address component that you want to extract and also the type. Refer to the API reference for the google.maps.places.PlaceResult class for information on address component and type. Our addressComponents object looks similar to this:

```
/* address components to retrieve */
var addressComponents = {
    street_number: 'short_name',
    route: 'long_name',
    locality: 'long_name',
    administrative_area_level_1: 'long_name',
    country: 'long_name',
    postal_code: 'short_name'
};
```

Next, we define the populateAddress method. As described earlier, this method takes the place object and the value of the addressAutoComplete binding as parameters. The method then extracts the address from place object and populates the model. Here is our implementation:

```
/* method to retrieve address information in the model */
var populateAddress = function (place, value) {

    var address = new AddressModel();
    //set location
    address.location(place.geometry.location);
    //loop through the components and extract required address
    fields
    for (var i = 0; i < place.address_components.length; i++) {
        var addressType = place.address_components[i].types[0];
        if (addressComponents[addressType]) {
            var val =
            place.address_components[i][addressComponents[addressType]];
            if (addressType == "street_number") {
                address.streetNumber(val);
            } else if (addressType == "route") {
                address.streetName(val);
            } else if (addressType == "locality") {
                address.city(val);
            } else if (addressType == "administrative_area_level_1") {
                address.state(val);
            } else if (addressType == "country") {
                address.country(val);
```

```
      } else if (addressType == "postal_code") {
        address.postCode(val);
      }
    }
  };
  //set the address model in the binding value
  value(address);
};
```

Modify the event listener in `addressAutoComplete` custom binding to call the
`populateAddress` method, like this:

```
/* custom binding for address auto complete */
ko.bindingHandlers.addressAutoComplete = {
  init: function(element, valueAccessor){
    // create the autocomplete object
    var autocomplete = new google.maps.places.Autocomplete(
    element,{ types: ['geocode'] });
    // when the user selects an address from the dropdown,
    populate the address in the model.
    var value = valueAccessor();
    google.maps.event.addListener(autocomplete, 'place_changed',
    function() {
      var place = autocomplete.getPlace();
      console.log(place);
      populateAddress(place, value);
    });
  }
};
```

Now that we have extracted the address information and populated our model, we
can now work on the view. Open the view in the `mapsapplication.html` file and
two panels side by side using the Bootstrap grid. The first panel is for displaying
`From address` and the second for `To address`. Display the address components
using the `text` binding from the model. Here is our implementation for displaying
from address:

```
<div class="panel panel-default">
  <div class="panel-heading">From address</div>
  <div class="panel-body" data-bind="with:
  MapsApplication.mapsModel.fromAddress">
    <div class="col-md-12" data-bind="visible: streetNumber">
      <strong>Street number: </strong>
      <span data-bind="text: streetNumber"> </span>
    </div>
    <div class="col-md-12" data-bind="visible: streetName">
```

```
       <strong>Street Name: </strong>
       <span data-bind="text: streetName"> </span>
    </div>
    <div class="col-md-12" data-bind="visible: city">
      <strong>City: </strong>
      <span data-bind="text: city"> </span>
    </div>
    <div class="col-md-12" data-bind="visible: postCode">
    <strong>Post code: </strong>
      <span data-bind="text: postCode"> </span>
    </div>
    <div class="col-md-12" data-bind="visible: country">
    <strong>Country: </strong>
      <span data-bind="text: country"> </span>
    </div>
    <div class="col-md-12" data-bind="visible: location()">
      <strong>Latitude: </strong>
      <span data-bind="text: location().lat()"> </span>
    </div>
    <div class="col-md-12" data-bind="visible: location()">
      <strong>Longitude: </strong>
      <span data-bind="text: location().lng()"> </span>
    </div>
  </div>
</div>
```

We have used the `with` binding to bind `fromAddress`. You can use the same code to display to address by simply changing the value of the `with` binding to `toAddress`.

Open the application in your browser and try selecting the from and to addresses. You should see the details of the address selected in the corresponding panels. In our browser, it looks similar to this:

We have reached our second checkpoint for this chapter. The code for this checkpoint can be found at `chapter9\checkpoint2`.

Rendering the map

The third feature is to about rendering the map in the view. To implement this feature, we will:

- Retrieve user location from the browser
- Create a custom binding handler for maps panel
- Update the view to display the map

Let's start by creating a method to retrieve the user location form the browser. The current user location information will be used to initialize the map. We will use the `getCurrentPosition` method of the `Geolocation` class provided by the browser to get the user's current location.

The `Geolocation` class provides methods to obtain the location of the device. The location information can be used to provide a customized experience to the user. The API reference for `Geolocation` class can be found at `https://developer.mozilla.org/en-US/docs/Web/API/Geolocation`.

Define an attribute to hold the user's current location, call it `localLocation`. Initialize this attribute with your local longitude and latitude:

```
var localLocation = {lat: -37.810432, lng: 144.96616};
```

The initial value is set in case the browser does not return the user's current location. Add a method to retrieve the user's location using the `Geolocation` class and update the `locaclLocation` attribute. Name this method `setLocalLocation`. Here is our implementation:

```
/* method to retrieve and set local location */
var setLocalLocation = function () {
  if ("geolocation" in navigator) {
    navigator.geolocation.getCurrentPosition(function(position) {
      localLocation.lat = position.coords.latitude;
      localLocation.lng = position.coords.longitude;
      console.log("successfully retrieved local location. Lat [" +
      localLocation.lat + "] Lng [" + localLocation.lng + "]");
    },
    function (error) {
      console.log("Could not get current coords: " +
      error.message);
    });
  };
};
```

Call this method from the `init` method of the module.

Next, we will create the custom binding to render a map in a panel. Create a custom binding called `mapPanel`. The `init` method of the binding should use the `google.maps.Map` class to render a map in the element provided:

```
/* custom binding handler for maps panel   */
ko.bindingHandlers.mapPanel = {
    init: function(element, valueAccessor){
        map = new google.maps.Map(element, {
          zoom: 10
        });
        centerMap(localLocation);
    }
};
```

Add this custom binding in the `configureBindingHandlers` method after the custom binding for `addressAutoComplete`. The `Map` class takes the HTML element and options as parameters. The only option we are setting is zoom. Refer to the API reference for more options. Note the call to the `centerMap` method. This method takes a `location` object as parameter and centers the map accordingly. It also triggers a resize:

```
/* method to center map based on the location*/
var centerMap = function (location) {
  map.setCenter(location);
  google.maps.event.trigger(map, 'resize');
}
```

Now that the custom binding for map panel has been defined, let's modify the view. Open the view in the `mapsapplication.html` file and add a panel at the end of the page. Give the panel an appropriate heading. Add a `div` element to the panel body and bind it to the custom binding we created to render a map. It should look similar to this:

```
<div class="row">
  <div class="col-md-12">
    <div class="panel panel-default">
      <div class="panel-heading">Map</div>
      <div class="panel-body">
        <div data-bind="mapPanel" class="map-canvas"></div>
      </div>
    </div>
  </div>
</div>
Define the style class map-canvas in the header of the page:
<head>
  ... ... ...
  <style>
    .map-canvas {
      width:100%;
      height:400px;
    }
  </style>
  ... ... ...
</head>
```

Open the application in your browser. You should now see a map displayed in the maps panel. In our browser, it should look similar to this:

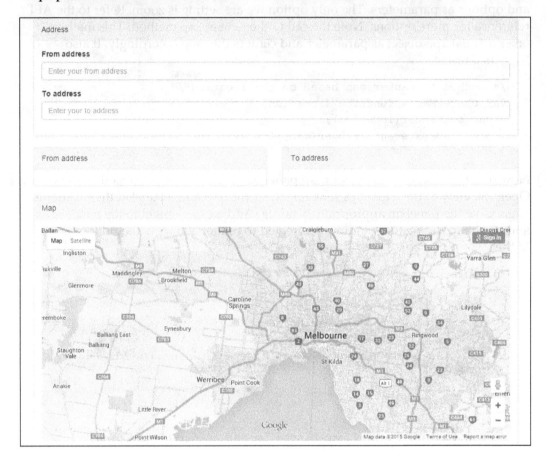

We have reached our third checkpoint for this chapter. The code for this checkpoint can be found at `chapter9\checkpoint3`.

Placing markers on the map

The fourth feature is about placing markers on the map for the selected addresses. To implement this feature, we will:

- Update the `address` model to hold the marker
- Create a method to place a marker on the map
- Create a method to remove an existing marker
- Register subscribers to trigger removal of the existing markers when an address changes
- Update the module to add a marker to the map

Let's get started by updating the `address` model. Open the `MapsApplication` module and locate the `AddressModel` variable. Add an observable to this model to hold the marker:

```
/* generic model for address */
var AddressModel = function() {
  this.marker = ko.observable();
  this.location = ko.observable();
  this.streetNumber = ko.observable();
  this.streetName = ko.observable();
  this.city = ko.observable();
  this.state = ko.observable();
  this.postCode = ko.observable();
  this.country = ko.observable();
};
```

Next, we will create a method that will create and place the marker on the map. This method should take `location` and `address` model as parameters. The method will also store the marker in the `address` model. Use the `google.maps.Marker` class to create and place the marker. Our implementation of this method looks similar to this:

```
/* method to place a marker on the map */
var placeMarker = function (location, value) {
  // create and place marker on the map
  var marker = new google.maps.Marker({
    position: location,
    map: map
  });
  //store the newly created marker in the address model
  value().marker(marker);
};
```

Now create a method that checks for an existing marker in the `address` model and removes it from the map. Name this method `removeMarker`. It should look similar to this:

```
/* method to remove old marker from the map */
var removeMarker = function(address) {
  if(address != null) {
    address.marker().setMap(null);
  }
};
```

Next step is to register subscribers that will trigger when an address changes. We will use these subscribers to trigger the removal of the existing markers. We will use the `beforeChange` event of the subscribers so that we have access to the existing markers in the model. Add subscribers to the `fromAddress` and `toAddress` observables to trigger the `beforeChange` event. Remove the existing markers on the trigger. To achieve this, I created a method called `registerSubscribers`. This method is called from the `init` method of the module. The method registers the two subscribers that triggers calls to `removeMarker`. Our implementation looks similar to this:

```
/* method to register subscriber */
var registerSubscribers = function () {
  //fire before from address is changed
  mapsModel.fromAddress.subscribe(function(oldValue) {
    removeMarker(oldValue);
  }, null, "beforeChange");

  //fire before to address is changed
  mapsModel.toAddress.subscribe(function(oldValue) {
    removeMarker(oldValue);
  }, null, "beforeChange");
};
```

We are now ready to bring the methods we created together and place a marker on the map. Create a map called `updateAddress`. This method should take two parameters: the place object and value binding. The method should call `populateAddress` to extract and populate the address model, and `placeMarker` to place a new marker on the map. Our implementation looks similar to this:

```
/* method to update the address model */
var updateAddress = function(place, value) {
  populateAddress(place, value);
  placeMarker(place.geometry.location, value);
};
```

Call the `updateAddress` method from the event listener in the `addressAutoComplete` custom binding:

```
google.maps.event.addListener(autocomplete, 'place_changed',
function() {
  var place = autocomplete.getPlace();
  console.log(place);
  updateAddress(place, value);
});
```

Open the application in your browser. Select **From address** and **To address**. You should now see markers appear for the two selected addresses. In our browser, the application looks similar to this:

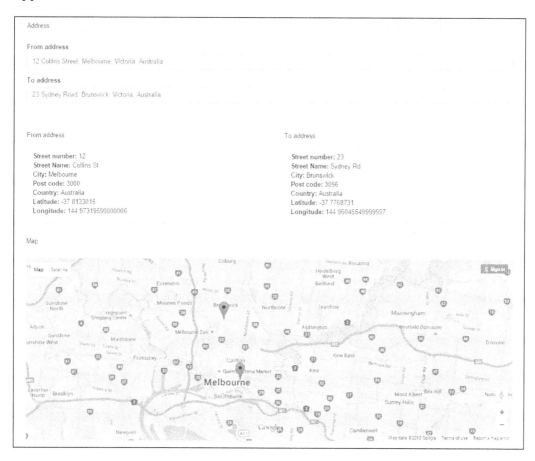

We have reached our fourth checkpoint for this chapter. The code for this checkpoint can be found at `chapter9\checkpoint4`.

Displaying route between markers

The last feature of the application is to draw a route between the two address markers. To implement this feature, we will:

- Create and initialize the direction service
- Request routing information from the direction service and draw the route
- Update the view to add a button to get directions

Let's get started by creating and initializing the direction service. We will use the `google.maps.DirectionsService` class to get the routing information and the `google.maps.DirectionsRenderer` class to draw the route on the map. Create two attributes in the `MapsApplication` module — one for directions service and the other for directions renderer:

```
/* the directions service */
var directionsService;
/* the directions renderer */
var directionsRenderer;
```

Next, create a method to create and initialize the preceding attributes:

```
/* initialize the direction service and display */
var initDirectionService = function () {
  directionsService = new google.maps.DirectionsService();
  directionsRenderer = new
  google.maps.DirectionsRenderer({suppressMarkers: true});
  directionsRenderer.setMap(map);
};
```

Call this method from the `mapPanel` custom binding handler after the map has been created and cantered. The updated `mapPanel` custom binding should look similar to this:

```
/* custom binding handler for maps panel */
ko.bindingHandlers.mapPanel = {
    init: function(element, valueAccessor){
      map = new google.maps.Map(element, {
        zoom: 10
      });
      centerMap(localLocation);
      initDirectionService();
    }
};
```

The next step is to create a method that will build and fire a request to the directions service to fetch the directions information. The direction information will then be used by the directions renderer to draw the route on the map. Our implementation of this method looks similar to this:

```
/* method to get directions and display route */
var getDirections = function () {
  //create request for directions
  var routeRequest = {
    origin: mapsModel.fromAddress().location(),
    destination: mapsModel.toAddress().location(),
    travelMode: google.maps.TravelMode.DRIVING
  };

  //fire request to route based on request
  directionsService.route(routeRequest, function(response, status)
{
    if (status == google.maps.DirectionsStatus.OK) {
      directionsRenderer.setDirections(response);
} else {
      console.log("No directions returned ...");
    }
  });
};
```

We created a routing request in the first part of the method. The request object consists of `origin`, `destination` and `travelMode`. The `origin` and `destination` is set to the locations for from and to addresses. The `travelMode` object is set to `google.maps.TravelMode.DRIVING`, which, as the name suggests, specifies that we require the driving route. Add the `getDirections` method to the `return` statement of the module as we will bind it to a button in the view.

One last step before we can work on the view is to clear the route on the map when the user selects a new address. This can be achieved by adding an instruction to clear the route information in the subscribers we registered earlier. Update the subscribers in the `registerSubscribers` method to clear the routes on the map:

```
/* method to register subscriber */
var registerSubscribers = function () {
  //fire before from address is changed
  mapsModel.fromAddress.subscribe(function(oldValue) {
    removeMarker(oldValue);
    directionsRenderer.set('directions', null);
```

```
    }, null, "beforeChange");

    //fire before to address is changed
    mapsModel.toAddress.subscribe(function(oldValue) {
        removeMarker(oldValue);
        directionsRenderer.set('directions', null);
    }, null, "beforeChange");
};
```

The last step is to update the view. Open the view and add a button under the address input components. Add `click` binding to the button and bind it to the `getDirections` method of the module. Add `enable` binding to make the button clickable only after the user has selected the two addresses. The button should look similar to this:

```
<button type="button" class="btn btn-default" data-bind="enable:
MapsApplication.mapsModel.fromAddress &&
MapsApplication.mapsModel.toAddress, click:
MapsApplication.getDirections">
    Get Directions
</button>
```

Open the application in your browser. Select **From address** and **To address**. The address details and markers should appear for the two selected addresses. Click on the **Get Directions** button. You should see the route drawn on the map between the two markers. In our browser, the application looks similar to this:

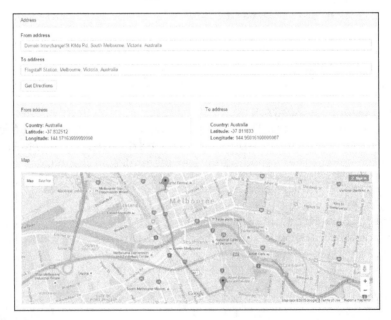

We have reached our last checkpoint for this chapter. The code for this checkpoint can be found at `chapter9\checkpoint5`.

Summary

In this chapter, we walked through building a map application using the Google Maps APIs. The application gave the users the ability to enter address information with `autocomplete` predictions based on partial address input, and retrieved and displayed detailed address information. It also rendered a map, placed markers based on the addresses selected, and displayed the route between the two markers.

We started the chapter by creating a reusable custom binding handler for the address `autocomplete` component. This custom binding was used to create from and to address components. The second feature of the application was to retrieve and display the detailed address information. We learned how to extract this information using the Google Maps APIs and store it in the Knockout observables.

In the third feature of the application, we created a reusable custom binding handler to render Google map in a panel. In the next two features, we learned how to place markers on the map and use the direction service to draw route between two markers. We learned how to use Knockout subscribers to interact with the map based on changes to the model.

We have reached the end of our journey with the conclusion of this chapter. Along the way, we explored the power of Knockout in developing rich, interactive, and modular web applications with an iterative development approach, sample code, and screenshots. We looked at the practical solutions to real-world problems including web forms, conditional validation, UI navigation, token-based security, CRUD operations, and integration with the Google Maps API. This brings our journey to a close. There has been a great deal of information and concepts to master, and we hope that the material in this book has made the journey easier for you.

Index

credit cards, validating 98-101
model validating, Knockout
    extenders used 82-84
model validating, Knockout validation
    plugin used 84
personal information, validating 87-91

E

eclipse
  URL 16
editable products grid application
  list of products, displaying 202-205
  products, adding 208-213
  products, deleting 206-208
  products, updating 213-216
  skeleton, creating 199-201

F

funds, customer banking portal
  functionality, adding to wizard 165-171
  transferring, between accounts 154
  transfers tab, creating 155, 156
  wizard component, creating 156-161

G

Google Group
  URL 27
Google Maps APIs
  address capturing, autocomplete feature
    used 222-226
  address details, capturing 227-231
  map, rendering 231-234
  marker, placing on map 235-237
  route between markers, displaying 238-241
  skeleton, creating 220-222

I

Integrated Development
    Environment (IDE) 16
Internet Engineering Task Force
  URL 174

J

jQuery
  URL 16
JSON 213
JSON Web Token (JWT) 174, 177

K

Knockout extenders
  used, for validating model 82-84
Knockout, features
  about 5
  automatic UI refresh 7, 8
  declarative bindings 5-7
  dependency tracking 8, 9
  templating 9-11
Knockout Home
  URL 27
Knockout validation plugin
  about 85
  address details, validating 94-98
  basics 86, 87
  contact details, validating 91-94
  credit cards, validating 98-101
  personal information, validating 87-91
  URL 84
  used, for validating model 84
Knockout GitHub
  URL 27

L

Learn Knockout
  URL 27
logged in user
  displaying 190, 191
login form
  validating 186-188

M

man-in-the middle attack 176
map, Google Maps APIs
  marker, placing 235-237
  rendering 231-234

model
  about 2
  validating, Knockout validation plugin
    used 84
  validating, Knockout extenders used 82-84
Model-View-View Model (MVVM) design
  pattern
  about 1, 2
  model 2, 3
  view 4, 5
  view model 3
module
  concept 11, 12
  initializing 13, 14
  merging 14, 15
  pattern 11
  private members 12, 13
  public members 12, 13

N

Node.js
  URL 16

O

OAuth 1.0a
  URL 174
OAuth 2.0
  URL 175
observables 7
online customer registration form
  about 51
  contact details, capturing 61-64
  credit card details, capturing 71-75
  features 51
  interests, capturing 76, 77
  personal information, capturing 55-61
  registration form, clearing 77-79
  residential address, capturing 65-71
  skeleton, creating 52-55
Open Web Application Security Project
  (OWASP)
  URL 176

R

Representational State Transfer (REST) 196

S

Secure Sockets Layer (SSL) 176
sever
  installing 197, 198
  running 197, 199
Stack Overflow
  URL 27

T

templating 9-11
to-do list application
  completed tasks, viewing 46-49
  features 30
  priority, setting for task 40-42
  skeleton, creating 30-32
  tasks, adding 32-35
  tasks, deleting 36, 37
  tasks, finishing 37-40
  tasks, sorting by name 43-45
  tasks, sorting by priority 43-45
  tasks, viewing 32-35
  total number of tasks, viewing 46-49
token-based authentication
  about 175
  JSON Web Token (JWT) 177
  versus, session in cookies 175, 176

U

Uniform Resource Identifiers (URIs) 196

V

validation
  adding, to customer registration
    form 81, 82
view 4, 5
view model 3

W

web server
  Apache HTTP Server 16
  Node.js HTTP Server 16
wireframe 107

Thank you for buying
KnockoutJS by Example

About Packt Publishing

Packt, pronounced 'packed', published its first book, *Mastering phpMyAdmin for Effective MySQL Management*, in April 2004, and subsequently continued to specialize in publishing highly focused books on specific technologies and solutions.

Our books and publications share the experiences of your fellow IT professionals in adapting and customizing today's systems, applications, and frameworks. Our solution-based books give you the knowledge and power to customize the software and technologies you're using to get the job done. Packt books are more specific and less general than the IT books you have seen in the past. Our unique business model allows us to bring you more focused information, giving you more of what you need to know, and less of what you don't.

Packt is a modern yet unique publishing company that focuses on producing quality, cutting-edge books for communities of developers, administrators, and newbies alike. For more information, please visit our website at www.packtpub.com.

About Packt Open Source

In 2010, Packt launched two new brands, Packt Open Source and Packt Enterprise, in order to continue its focus on specialization. This book is part of the Packt Open Source brand, home to books published on software built around open source licenses, and offering information to anybody from advanced developers to budding web designers. The Open Source brand also runs Packt's Open Source Royalty Scheme, by which Packt gives a royalty to each open source project about whose software a book is sold.

Writing for Packt

We welcome all inquiries from people who are interested in authoring. Book proposals should be sent to author@packtpub.com. If your book idea is still at an early stage and you would like to discuss it first before writing a formal book proposal, then please contact us; one of our commissioning editors will get in touch with you.

We're not just looking for published authors; if you have strong technical skills but no writing experience, our experienced editors can help you develop a writing career, or simply get some additional reward for your expertise.

KnockoutJS Web Development

ISBN: 978-1-78216-102-8   Paperback: 178 pages

Efficiently work with data, web templates, and custom HTML tags using KnockoutJS

1. Simplify page logic with automated calculations and control the visibility of your CSS elements with the help of robust yet friendly templates.

2. Create your own custom HTML tags that provide dynamic interactive logic using meaningful markup naming conventions and structures.

3. Use best practices to work with simple as well as complex data that interacts with your view components.

KnockoutJS Blueprints

ISBN: 978-1-78398-084-0   Paperback: 218 pages

Learn how to design and create amazing web applications using KnockoutJS

1. Create fully testable web applications from real-world solutions with the powerful data-binding offered by KnockoutJS.

2. Create new and reusable components by yourself and learn how to integrate external libraries easily.

3. Contains projects based on fictitious, but common, application development briefs.

Please check **www.PacktPub.com** for information on our titles

Mastering KnockoutJS

ISBN: 978-1-78398-100-7   Paperback: 270 pages

Use and extend Knockout to deliver feature-rich, modern web applications

1. Customize Knockout to add functionality and integrate with third-party libraries.

2. Create full web applications using binding preprocessors, Node preprocessors, and the Knockout Punches library.

3. In a step-by-step manner, explore the Knockout ecosystem by looking at popular plugins as well as the Durandal Framework.

KnockoutJS Essentials

ISBN: 978-1-78439-707-4   Paperback: 232 pages

Implement a successful JavaScript-rich application with KnockoutJS, jQuery, and Bootstrap

1. Create rich Internet applications using JavaScript.

2. In a step-by-step manner, explore how to customize and extend KnockoutJS to take your app to the next level.

3. Great examples show how KnockoutJS can simplify your code and make it more robust.

Please check **www.PacktPub.com** for information on our titles